AUTONOMIA:
Its Genesis and Early History

THE AMERICAN PHILOLOGICAL ASSOCIATION

AMERICAN CLASSICAL STUDIES

edited by
Deborah Samuel

NUMBER 11

AUTONOMIA:
Its Genesis and Early History

Martin Ostwald

MARTIN OSTWALD

AUTONOMIA:
Its Genesis and Early History

SCHOLARS PRESS

AUTONOMIA:
Its Genesis and Early History

Martin Ostwald

© 1982
The American Philological Association

Library of Congress Cataloging in Publication Data
Ostwald, Martin, 1922–
  Autonomia, its genesis and early history.

  (American classical studies ; no. 11) (ISSN 0278–5943)
  Includes index.
  1. Athens—Foreign relations. 2. Athens—Politics and government. 3. Delian League, First, 5th century, B.C. 4. Autonomy—History. I. Title. II. Series.
JC79.A8083   327.38'5   82-5768
ISBN 0-89130-572-6   AACR2

Printed in the United States of America

FOR LORE

TABLE OF CONTENTS

	Page
PREFACE	ix
TEXT	1
NOTES	51
BIBLIOGRAPHY	71
INDEX LOCORUM	75

PREFACE

The present monograph was originally conceived as an appendix to a larger book on the internal workings of the Athenian democracy in the fifth century B.C. In examining the reciprocal effect of imperial power on internal politics, I soon realized the central importance of the concept of *autonomia* in determining the relationship between the Athenians and their allies, and with this realization the intended appendix assumed a life of its own. From the fundamental article published by the late E. J. Bickerman in 1958, I learned that *autonomia* belongs to the vocabulary of interstate relationships. My debt to him will be evident to most of my readers. I then discovered that the development and meaning of the concept can only be seen in the general context of the most important terms used by the Greeks to describe the sanctions which regulate different kinds of relations between states. My conclusion, that *autonomia* was coined to express a relationship for which no other term was available, is argued in the following pages.

Many friends and colleagues have given unstintingly of their expertise, time, and effort to make this book better in conception and execution than it originally was. Foremost among them are David Asheri, Paul A. Cartledge, John K. Davies, Miriam T. Griffin, Russell Meiggs, and Oswyn Murray. What shortcomings and errors it still has are entirely mine.

The essential outline of this monograph was completed during a year's leave in Oxford in 1977-78, which was made possible by the award of a fellowship from the J. S. Guggenheim Memorial Foundation and the generous leave policy of Swarthmore College. To Swarthmore College I am also indebted for a liberal subvention to defray some of the costs of publication, and to the Editorial Board for Monographs of the American Philological Association, its chairman, Professor Deborah H. Samuel, and its anonymous readers for accepting it for publication.

Thanks of a different kind are due to my colleagues at Swarthmore College, especially Helen North, and at the University of Pennsylvania, for providing the stimulating environment which makes classical scholarship the delight that it is. A debt which cannot be repaid is acknowledged in the dedication.

Swarthmore College and
University of Pennsylvania
  February 1982

Αὐτονομία: ITS GENESIS AND EARLY HISTORY

That αὐτονομία is one of the key concepts for an understanding of the relation between Athens and her allies in the Delian League cannot be questioned. The role it played in the debates and embassies immediately preceding the Peloponnesian War is familiar from Thucydides,[1] and its meaning in that context has been explored in a brilliant and fundamental study by E. J. Bickerman.[2] It is the great merit of his work to have established that αὐτονομία differs from ἐλευθερία in being a concept in interstate relations, in that the independence of the "autonomous" state stands always in the shadow of a stronger power.[3] This leads him to believe that the concept originated in Asia Minor where it was coined to express the status granted the Greek cities under Persian rule.[4] Admittedly there is no direct evidence, and the etymological argument based on the derivation from αὐτός + νέμειν, apart from being substantively questionable, does not get us very far.[5] Moreover, Herodotus, our best authority for the relations between the Asiatic Greek cities and the Persians, does not even once use the αὐτονομ-stem to describe this relationship.

The purpose of the present investigation is, therefore, to reopen the question of the origin of the concept of αὐτονομία on the basis of Bickerman's demonstration that it belongs to the vocabulary of inter-state relations. Since, as we shall see, it is always used of a weaker state which tries to assert its independence in the face of a major power, but never of the independence of the stronger power, our thesis is that αὐτονομία developed in an attempt by weaker states to find constraints with which to inhibit the exercise of power by a stronger state over them. We further believe that the relationship expressed by αὐτονομία first came into existence with the development of the Delian League into an Athenian Empire, and that the concept was coined by Athenian allies in protest against the more unpleasant manifestations of the Athenian ἀρχή. In short, we hope to show that αὐτονομία came into being as part of an attempt to find sanctions against the arbitrary use of force by a major state against minor states moving in its orbit.

I

The problem of finding effective sanctions was in antiquity as in our own time the most serious obstacle to defining efficient rules for the conduct of inter-state relations. Within a particular state, νόμος, when unqualified, expressed the prevailing rules adherence to which could be enforced by the organs entrusted with the administration of justice. The absence of an enforcing agency --short of armed force--in relations between states made the unqualified use of νόμος unsuitable for expressing the rules by which these relations could be regulated,[6] and, except for those cases in which arbitration procedures could be agreed upon in advance, sanctions had to be found in the nebulous realm of traditions, religion, a common heritage, a common humanity, or similar terms whose vagueness made the ultimate arbiter the sensibilities or perceptions of one or both of the affected parties--a very weak sanction indeed. The vocabulary for these sanctions was usually borrowed from the vocabulary describing those social, religious, or behavioral rules within a given state which cannot be, or are not primarily thought of as, judicially enforceable. For example, various kinds of qualified νόμοι and νόμιμα are invoked to describe usages of war, mainly in allegations that they have been infringed by an opponent or in defence of one's own actions against recriminations. Thus the right to defend oneself against an attacker is described as a universal human law by the Plataeans in Thucydides (3.56.2), and the Thebans concede that it is κατά νόμον τινά to kill one's opponent in battle (3.66.2). Herodotus (7.136.2) has Xerxes accuse the Spartans of having violated τά πάντων ἀνθρώπων νόμιμα in having slain the heralds whom he had despatched to them. More frequently, such usages are described as sanctioned by or as applicable to the Greeks alone: the Ἑλλήνων νόμος frowns upon an attack launched without provocation (Thucydides 3.67.6), it does not condone the slaughter of a captive taken in battle (Euripides, *Heracleidai* 1009-11), especially if he has surrendered voluntarily (Thucydides 3.58.3; 59.1), and, while the Athenians affirm, the Boeotians deny the Greek law that a sanctuary belongs to the power occupying and controlling the territory in which it is situated (Thucydides 4.97.2-3; 98.2). A valuable insight into the conduct expected from Greek by Greek is afforded by the δικαιώματα ἱκανά κατά τούς Ἑλλήνων νόμους, "points sufficient in terms of the code of the Greeks to justify," as the Corinthians believe, their representations against acceptance by the Athenians of an alliance with Corcyra (Thucydides 1.41.1). Among these points are the refusal of Corcyra to submit the case against Epidamnus to arbitration before laying siege to the city; Corcyra's request for an alliance with Athens at a time when things went badly for her; the

deleterious effect which acceptance of a Corcyrean alliance by
Athens would have on the Thirty-Years' Peace; and finally, the
priority of good relations between Athens and Corinth over good
relations with Corcyra. But the "Greek laws" seem to have had a
less strong hold upon the Athenians: the only effect of the
δικαιώματα on them was to make them more inclined than they had
been before to accept the Corcyreans into a defensive alliance
(Thucydides 1.44.1). Similarly, the καθεστὸς τοῖς ῝Ελλησι νόμιμον
to regard as traitors those who switch from one alliance to another
does not deter the Mytilenians who cite it to appeal to Sparta for
help in their planned revolt against Athens (Thucydides 3.9.1).

The fact that τὰ κοινὰ τῶν ῝Ελλήνων νόμιμα and οἱ ῝Ελλήνων
νόμοι have no place in any of the treaties between states that have
come down to us indicates that their sanction was not a solid
enough basis for a compact and lent itself more readily to pious
platitudes used by one state in arguing with another. In documents we find in their place appeals to τὰ πάτρια or πάτριοι νόμοι,
traditions thought of as binding by and on all or a substantial
section of the Greeks. A discussion of them will lead us straight
into a preliminary definition of αὐτονομία.

These documentary uses of πάτριος are found primarily in
treaties or parts of treaties which deal with religious matters
and in arbitration clauses.[7] A basic feature of every truce is
that each side permits the other to take up its dead κατὰ τὰ
πάτρια once the truce has become effective (Thucydides 4.98.8),
suggesting that religion is the sanction behind τὰ πάτρια. This
is corroborated by the fact that the initial clauses of both the
one-year armistice between Athens and Sparta of 423 B.C. and of
the Peace of Nicias of 421 B.C. invoke the πάτριοι νόμοι and τὰ
πάτρια, respectively, to guarantee free access to religious
shrines.[8] Further, the one-year armistice also invokes the πάτριοι νόμοι to bring to justice those who had helped themselves to
monies belonging to Apollo, presumably by applying the laws
against ἱεροσυλία prevailing in Athens and Sparta,[9] while τὰ πάτρια in the Peace of Nicias also guarantee the complete political,
fiscal, and juridical independence of Delphi.[10] Both these latter
cases assume that πάτρια can be enforced by a court of law, and
that the decision of that court will be legally binding upon all
Greeks.

Of substantive political significance is also the sanction of
τὰ πάτρια in arbitration clauses. Again, the one-year armistice
of 423 B.C. provides an example in the mutual promise of both

parties δίκας τε διδόναι ὐμᾶς τε ἡμῖν καὶ ἡμᾶς ὑμῖν κατὰ τὰ πάτρια, τὰ ἀμφίλογα δίκῃ διαλύοντας ἄνευ πολέμου.[11] That the Athenians subsequently refused to have the defection of Skione, when it tokk place two days later, submitted to arbitration need not concern us here,[12] beyond pointing out that arbitration clauses are always in jeopardy when there is no third party more powerful than the contracting parties to enforce them. But what kind of sanctions are envisaged by κατὰ τὰ πάτρια, especially since the most recent arbitration clause between the Athenians and Lacedaemonians, that of the Thirty-Years' Peace,[13] had become a dead letter with the outbreak of the Peloponnesian War almost a decade earlier?[14] Some scholars have remarked that the truce does not spell out the details of arbitration procedure.[15] But since Greek treaties usually tend not to be specific on this point and assume the practice of appointing a third party to arbitrate the peaceful settlement of disputes between states,[16] κατὰ τὰ πάτρια seems to refer to this general practice as the "traditional ways" short of war in which disputes were normally expected to be settled in the Greek world. It is noteworthy that the phrase was abandoned in the arbitration clause of the Peace of Nicias two years later and a more realistic "mutual agreement" in establishing arbitration procedures substituted for it.[17]

The πάτρια which sanction arbitration clauses in treaties among Peloponnesian states, even when these were not members of the Peloponnesian League, are of special interest not only in that they refer to traditions apparently thought of as confined to the Peloponnese, but also because they relate τὰ πάτρια to αὐτονομία. Our evidence consists of the fifty-year peace treaty concluded between Sparta and the Argive oligarchy in 418/17 B.C. preceded by a ξυμβατήριος λόγος, presented by the Spartan Lichas as a resolution passed by the Spartan assembly. This resolution anticipates the guarantee of independence of *all* Peloponnesian cities, which will later form part of the alliance: τὰς δὲ πόλιας τὰς ἐν Πελοποννάσῳ, καὶ μικρὰς καὶ μεγάλας, αὐτονόμως ἦμεν πάσας καττὰ πάτρια.[18] The two contracting major powers guarantee the αὐτονομία of all Peloponnesian cities on the basis of πάτρια which, one must assume, here denotes the principle on which the Peloponnesian cities traditionally expected to deal with one another. That these πάτρια are confined to the Peloponnese is suggested by the fact that they do not form part of that section of the Spartan resolution which regulates the relations of the contracting parties with their allies outside the Peloponnese.[19]

This brings us to the three arbitration clauses of the treaty itself, which are not included in the Spartan resolution. Each of these contains the phrase καττὰ πάτρια, but in each it is invoked to sanction something different. In the first clause, πάτρια sanction the arbitration procedure with the words ἐπὶ τοῖς ἴσοις καὶ ὁμοίοις δίκας διδόντας καττὰ πάτρια.[20] This may well be a Peloponnesian equivalent of the phrase δίκας τε διδόναι ὑμᾶς τε ἡμῖν καὶ ἡμᾶς ὑμῖν in the one-year armistice,[21] while καττὰ πάτρια may refer to the ethnic solidarity which the Dorians of the Peloponnese ideally expected themselves to feel for one another. In the second clause, which invites other Peloponnesian cities to join the alliance, the πάτρια guarantee the integrity of the territory of each: ταὶ δὲ ἄλλαι πόλιες ταὶ ἐν Πελοποννάσῳ κοινανεόντω τᾶν σπονδᾶν καὶ τᾶς ξυμμαχίας αὐτόνομοι καὶ αὐτοπόλιες, τὰν αὐτῶν ἔχοντες καττὰ πάτρια, δίκας διδόντες τὰς ἴσας καὶ ὁμοίας.[22] How are we to explain the shift of καττὰ πάτρια from the arbitration clause to the clause guaranteeing territorial integrity? Earlier in Thucydides, the Corinthian request to the Argives after the Peace of Nicias to take over the leadership of the Peloponnese uses a willingness "to submit to fair and impartial judicial proceedings" as a characteristic of any αὐτόνομος πόλις: any Greek city so desiring, ἥτις αὐτόνομός τέ ἐστι καὶ δίκας ἴσας καὶ ὁμοίας δίδωσι, is invited to enter into a defensive alliance with Argos.[23] Now, the αὐτονομία of the Peloponnesian cities is also recognized in the treaty between Argos and Sparta under discussion. But here the adjective αὐτοπόλιες which is not found again in Greek literature, is joined with αὐτόνομοι, evidently to make the point that all Peloponnesian cities, whether they are members of the Peloponnesian League or not, should relinquish their sovereignty over other Peloponnesian cities as, for example, Mantineia over the Arcadian cities she had annexed, including Parrhasia, which the Spartans had made αὐτονόμους, and Elis over Lepreon whose citizens Spartan arbitrators had declared to be αὐτονόμους.[24] In the context of these stipulations, καττὰ πάτρια makes special sense when it is attached to the declaration of the territorial integrity of each Peloponnesian city, and when τὰν αὐτῶν ἔχοντες καττὰ πάτρια reinforces the αὐτονομία guaranteed each city as an individual unit (αὐτοπόλιες) in the preceding words. It strengthens and makes specific the proposal submitted in the Spartan resolution, which required Peloponnesian cities small and large αὐτονόμως ἦμεν πάσας καττὰ πάτρια, without adding καττὰ πάτρια to τὰν αὐτῶν ἔχοντες.[25] In other words, the recognition of the territorial integrity of each Peloponnesian city (αὐτοπόλιες) is here associated with its recognition as an αὐτόνομος unit and is guaranteed by history, that is by the traditional ancestral ways.

The third invocation of τὰ πάτρια in the final clause of the treaty is less relevant to our immediate purposes. It makes provision for the settlement of disputes among any members of the alliance, both Peloponnesian and non-Peloponnesian signatories, in two respects:[26] third cities to be agreed upon by the contending parties are to arbitrate all disputes, while disputes among individual citizens of different allied states are to be adjudicated καττὰ πάτρια, that is, presumably by proceedings established between particular member-states.[27] In sum, "tradition" is invoked in the treaty between Argos and Sparta to sanction (a) arbitration as the way of settling public differences, (b) the right of all independent cities to their territory, and (c) procedures enshrined in treaties among member-states for the settlement of disputes among their citizens.

Our discussion of the place of τὰ πάτρια in relations between states has shown that it serves to provide, if not a firm sanction, yet at least a reminder to the states involved that certain traditions, which should not be broken, represented a norm in interstate relations. Those sanctions of τὰ πάτρια which rest on religious sensibilities were, as we saw, strong enough to guarantee the inviolability of panhellenic sanctuaries and, in the form of πάτριοι νόμοι, could be enforced by tribunals whose verdicts all Greek states were expected to accept. In arbitration clauses, on the other hand, where the appeal to πάτρια applies the sanction of no more than a common heritage or a common tradition, much will have depended on whether the contending parties were able to agree upon an arbitrator and, if so, to accept his verdict.

The result most relevant to our present purposes is, however, the relation we noted between τὰ πάτρια and αὐτονομία which, since we found it in contexts which do not involve Athens' relation to her allies and in documentary language, give us a more objective framework for our preliminary definition of the concept. Two conclusions can be drawn from the ξυμβατήριος λόγος submitted to Argos in 418/17 B.C. In the first place, the proposal that Sparta and Argos let the small and large cities of the Peloponnese αὐτονόμως ἦμεν πάσας καττὰ πάτρια (Thucydides 5.77.5) shows that αὐτονομία is regarded as the normal traditional status to which the states to whom it is applied are believed to be historically entitled, and secondly, in the present instance at least, it is not the states involved which proclaim themselves as αὐτονόμως, but the recognition of their αὐτονομία is proposed by Sparta as a subject of agreement between herself and Argos. The most remarkable fact is that the αὐτονομία of the two major contracting powers is neither proclaimed nor even mentioned, although it is of course included in the general point that *all* cities of the Peloponnese shall be αὐτονόμως. In other words, αὐτονομία is taken for granted by the major powers for themselves, but it is explicitly conceded to all other Peloponnesian cities in the form of a guarantee of their political integrity.

That it is the political integrity which is at issue is corroborated by the other two passages which associate αὐτόνομος with τὰ πάτρια. The clause in the Peace of Nicias which guarantees the integrity of the sanctuary as well as of the city of Delphi κατὰ τὰ πάτρια is the most emphatic piece of evidence in that it adds αὐτοτελεῖς καὶ αὐτοδίκους to αὐτονόμους and extends the guarantee of integrity to the people as well as the territory of Delphi.[28] Since αὐτοτελεῖς includes the injunction that Delphi must pay tribute to neither a superior power nor to a confederacy but be left to determine the disposal of her finances without outside interference, and since αὐτοδίκους guarantees freedom from external interference in the administration of justice at Delphi, αὐτονόμους--although it is of course strengthened by the addition of these two adjectives--evidently guarantees the freedom of the people of Delphi to make their political decisions without external interference. Further, the extension of the guarantee of territorial integrity is here a condition of αὐτονομία, since it can be related neither to payment of tribute nor to the administration of justice. The emphatic and specific nature of the guarantee, expressed in the three adjectives, leaves no doubt that it was dictated by historical circumstances, particularly the frequent encroachment by the Phocians on Delphic territory.[29] But this pedantic specificity enables us to see that, closely related though the three terms are, a form of αὐτονομία can be envisaged which does involve the payment of tribute and which does affect the administration of justice: for if αὐτονόμους excluded by definition the payment of tribute and automatically guaranteed the functioning of the lawcourts free from the interference of an external power, there would have been no need for the addition of αὐτοτελεῖς and αὐτοδίκους. Finally, this clause of the Nicias Peace confirms what the ξυμβατήριος λόγος of 5.77.5 has already taught us, namely that αὐτονομία is not something which major powers claim for themselves but it is a concession or a recognition which they extend to states less powerful than themselves.

The addition of αὐτοπόλιες to αὐτόνομοι in the description of the Peloponnesian cities to be invited to join the Spartan-Argive alliance is, as we have seen, also due to the special political situation on the Peloponnese in 418/17 B.C.[30] This situation adds special poignancy to the guarantee of territorial inviolability sanctioned by τὰ πάτρια, which seems to form part of the recognition of the political integrity of each city. There is one further element of αὐτονομία which we can learn from this passage, namely the capacity to render "fair and impartial judicial proceedings"--δίκας διδόντες τὰς ἴσας καὶ ὁμοίας. That this capacity is a characteristic of any αὐτόνομος πόλις is, as we have seen, confirmed by the Corinthian proposal to the Argives of 421 B.C., where it is couched in the same terms.[31] It is not identical with the right guaranteed by the term αὐτόδικοι to the Delphians in the Peace of Nicias, which is evidently applicable only to Delphi's handling of its own internal juridical affairs and refers to the settlement of disputes between individuals. The phrase δίκας τὰς ἴσας καὶ ὁμοίας διδόναι, on the other hand, appears as a proviso rather than as a right: states are admitted into or invited to join an alliance on condition that they render "fair and impartial judicial proceedings," evidently to ensure that outstanding issues will be arbitrated rather than become a cause of war.[32] It is a feature of relations between states and not of internal politics. What relates it to αὐτονομία is presumably the fact that it constitutes an understanding not to resort to force so long as an issue can be settled by peaceful arbitration. The promise to give δίκας ἴσας καὶ ὁμοίας is, therefore, one way in which powerful states are--in principle at least--placed on a footing of equality with their weaker treaty partners. This says of course nothing about the reality behind the profession: when the Spartans and Argives, after promising αὐτονομία to the Peloponnesian cities, immediately imposed it on the cities dominated by Mantineia, and proceeded to establish oligarchies in Sicyon and Achaea and to stage a shortlived oligarchical revolt at Argos,[33] they did little more than follow precedents set earlier by the Athenians. The trouble is of course that no professions of equality can prevent the more powerful party to an alliance from coercing its weaker partner.

The documents we have so far discussed, sc. the Peace of Nicias of 421 B.C. and the Spartan-Argive alliance of 418/17 B.C., preceded by the ξυμβατήριος λόγος, are the only places in which a sanction behind αὐτονομία is mentioned: τὰ πάτρια, traditions recognized as such, are the only guarantee of independence a weaker state can rely on when it is faced with the superior power of a strong state. From the point of view of the weak state, αὐτονομία is, therefore, not much more than a plea that a strong state should respect the independence which it has traditionally enjoyed in the Greek world. The fact that major powers do not proclaim their αὐτονομία but concede it to or recognize it in minor powers underlines that it is no more than a plea, in that from the viewpoint of the major power it is simply a declaration of its willingness to refrain from exercizing the power it has, a willingness which is in the control of the major power alone and depends on the historical circumstances in which it finds itself at any given time. If the guarantee of αὐτονομία extended to them by Sparta and Argos put the smaller Peloponnesian cities at rest, it did not do so for long.

We are also in a position to make some preliminary observations on what constitutes αὐτονομία in these documents. Both the Peace of Nicias and the Spartan-Argive alliance agree in treating it as political independence, even if the Peace of Nicias subsumes also territorial integrity under it, while the Spartan-Argive alliance found it necessary to differentiate between the two. The Peace of Nicias also suggests that payment of tribute to a major power is not irreconcilable with an αὐτόνομος status and that some interference in internal jurisdiction can be tolerated. This is corroborated by a clause in that treaty which we will have to discuss again later, and which suggests that payment of tribute was the only thing which stood between some allied cities and the loss of their αὐτονομία.[34] And finally, αὐτονομία seems in some instances to be contingent upon the willingness to "render fair and impartial judicial proceedings" when it came to submit matters to arbitration; but here, too, the burden was on the weak states, for they had no redress when a major power refused to submit to arbitration.

II

With this preface on sanctions, we must now turn to the questions of origin and meaning which, we may assume, will be closely linked to one another. On the question of its etymology, we have made some remarks already, and our preliminary observations enable us to surmise that the νομος-suffix is less likely to refer to statutes than to the source which issues and guarantees norms,[35] i.e., describing as "autonomous" a state which is free to determine the norms by which it wants to live. The concept αὐτονομία is not attested in writings before the second half of the fifth century. This may of course be due merely to the accident that no earlier passage containing it has been preserved. Bickerman seems to subscribe to this view when he conjectures that the term originated in Asia Minor to describe the relation of the Greek cities to their Persian overlords in the sixth century.[36] Support for it can be drawn from three passages in the Hippocratic treatise *On Airs, Waters, and Places*, to be discussed presently, in which αὐτονομία is predicated of Greek cities living in the shadow of superior Asiatic powers. However, the treatise describes a situation prevailing in the fifth century, and it remains strange that Herodotus never applies the term to the relationship of the Asiatic Greeks to their eastern neighbors in his discussion of the development of this relationship in the sixth century, although he uses the term elsewhere. In view of that, it is safer to a fifth-century origin for the concept about the time at which it is first attested, and further, its close relation to τὰ πάτρια may suggest that it arose to describe a relationship among Greek states rather than of Greek to non-Greek states. All this points to a development of the concept in the period which culminated in the outbreak of the Peloponnesian War, when the development of the two powerblocks, Athens and Sparta, after the end of the Persian Wars, deprived smaller states of rights which they had taken for granted from time immemorial as theirs κατὰ τὰ πάτρια. In literature, the concept is found far more frequently in Thucydides, the only surviving historian of that period, than in any other author, most commonly in the adjectival form αὐτόνομος, more rarely in the noun form αὐτονομία and the verb form αὐτονομέομαι, and never in the fifth century as an adverb.[37]

The earliest datable occurrence of the adjective (441 B.C.) is at once the most problematic in that it constitutes the only surviving example of the fifth century in which it describes a personal quality rather than the condition of a state, and in that its contextual meaning is not free from difficulties. As Antigone proceeds to her rocky tomb, the Chorus comments that her death will come not by disease or by sword, ἀλλ' αὐτόνομος ζῶσα μόνη δὴ / θνατῶν Ἀίδαν καταβήσῃ.[38] Jebb's interpretation of this passage as glorifying Antigone as "mistress of <her> own fate," whom "no one constrained...to do the act for which she suffers" and who "knew that death would be the consequence, and she chose it,"[39] has rightly been attacked by B.M.W. Knox, who argues convincingly that "the chorus shows no sympathy and places the full responsibility for her imminent death on her own head," because she "lives by her own law."[40] In the context of the play this means that Antigone has put herself outside the pale of the νόμοι of the city and has defied them by making the ἄγραπτα κἀσφαλῆ θεῶν νόμιμα her own without letting the laws of the city influence her decision to bury her brother: the tone of lines 821-22 is no different from the Chorus' charge at line 875: σὲ δ' αὐτόγνωτος ὤλεσ' ὀργά--"The temper underlying your self-made decision has ruined you."

The uniqueness of this passage makes any interpretation little more than guesswork, because no parallels for a personal use of αὐτόνομος can be adduced. Yet this circumstance also enables us to assert with some confidence that Sophocles is using the adjective in this passage not in its primary but in a metaphorical sense. For since all other attested uses of αὐτόνομος carry a political meaning, we may assume that the political is the original connotation, which must have been sufficiently well entrenched in Attic usage by 441 B.C. to enable the poet to give it a metaphorical personal sense intelligible and acceptable to his audience. We can go a step further: regardless of the interpretation accepted, αὐτόνομος is here not a right conceded or recognized by a major power to its inferior, as it was in the passages so far discussed, but it describes a quality as having been arrogated by an individual in defiance of the superior power of the state. In other words, even though the state has not conceded αὐτονομία to Antigone, it is in relation to its superior power that she is seen as αὐτόνομος. It is important to note, however, that the quality is predicated by an outsider, in this case the Chorus, and it remains doubtful whether Antigone would have proudly professed her defiance of Creon's νόμοι by describing herself as αὐτόνομος, just as she would certainly not have herself described her act as αὐτόγνωτος. In short, αὐτόνομος here is a quality "objectively" predicated by others; it is not a quality "subjectively" claimed by an individual as an inalienable or natural right with which he has been endowed by his Creator.[41]

The content of αὐτόνομος in the *Antigone* includes at once a recognition and a denial of the claims of a higher authority, here those of the state. The same tendency can be observed in the political use of the adjective in three passages of the Hippocratic treatise *On Airs, Waters, and Places*, where it is opposed to

despotism, expressed by the verbs βασιλεύομαι or δεσπόζομαι.⁴²
The context makes it clear that the despotism to which it is opposed is envisaged as the domination of Greek city-states by Asiatic powers; it is not envisaged as the rule of one man within a city-state. In other words, αὐτόνομος describes primarily, though not exclusively, the quality of those Greek cities in Asia Minor which, though they live in the shadow of a superior power which potentially threatens their existence, still enjoy a degree of self-determination and independence of which despotism has deprived the Asiatics.⁴³ This explains why the positive attitudes of αὐτόνομοι-peoples are precisely those of which subjugation by a superior power would deprive them: control over their own social and political life, the enjoyment of the fruits of their own labor, and embarking on hazardous enterprises only when these will bring benefits to one's own society.⁴⁴ If we compare these characteristics of being αὐτόνομος with those we have already encountered, it is possible to say, though perhaps more subtle than the text warrants, that the term here includes the αὐτοτελεῖς which was separately mentioned in the Peace of Nicias, since the enjoyment of the fruits of one's labors precludes the payment of tribute to an outside power,⁴⁵ and that it suggests freedom of interference in the internal affairs of a state by a stronger external power, inasmuch as coerced participation in dangerous enterprises, such as military expeditions, is incompatible with assuming only those risks from which one's own society stands to gain. Further, as in the *Antigone*, the αὐτόνομος status is not conceded or granted by a superior power but it is seen with reference to it. It is a purely descriptive term, but with somewhat more positive overtones than it has in the *Antigone*.

Opposition of αὐτονομία to the kind of one-man rule common in Asia is evident also in Herodotus' narrative of the rise of Deioces: ἐόντων δὲ αὐτονόμων πάντων ἀνὰ τὴν ἤπειρον ὧδε αὖτις ἐς τυραννίδας περιῆλθον.⁴⁶ Since we are told that the Medes lived settled in villages (κατὰ κώμας), we may assume that with the fall of a central authority each village regained that independent status which was originally and traditionally its own, a status envisaged with reference to the superior power of Assyria which had earlier denied the villages their independence, and which will be denied again with Deioces' establishment of kingship (Herodotus 1.97.3-98.1): αὐτονομία cannot be reconciled with τυραννίς. As in Sophocles and [Hippocrates] it is the description of a status possessed and recognized as such by a major power.

This descriptive use of αὐτόνομος to define the political independence of small settlements with the implication that this independence is contingent on the tolerance of a larger power is common also in Thucydides. He uses the adjective to describe, for example, the political status which the various settlements scattered throughout the countryside of Attica enjoyed before the synoecism, which looms in the background,[47] as he uses it also of many Thracian settlements mentioned in his narrative of Sitalces' expedition against Macedonia. The establishment of a kingdom of the Odrysians over a larger part of Thrace by Sitalces' father Teres is said to have been the earliest attempt of its kind among the Thracians, remarkable in that a large part of Thrace is αὐτόνομον.[48] The situation described corresponds closely to that which Deioces found among the Medes: although Thrace consisted largely of independently governed units, Teres succeeded in establishing his dominion over them, an act which, we may assume, spelled the end of local αὐτονομία for the affected settlements in much the same way in which the Median κῶμαι ceased to be αὐτόνομοι when Deioces established his kingship. That αὐτονομία, while implying the existence of a larger power in the background, excludes domination by it (ἀρχή) is shown in the account of Sitalces' levy of troops for his Macedonian expedition. Of his own Odrysians and of the other tribes ὧν ἦρχε it is said that he "raised" them (ἀνίστησιν), while he "invited" (παρεκάλει) many of the αὐτόνομοι mountain dwellers of Thrace to join him as mercenaries or as volunteers; also, the boundaries of his dominion (ἀρχή) are defined by describing as αὐτονόμους the peoples who live unsubjugated on the other side of them.[49] Thucydides' account shows not only, as Bickerman has pointed out, that αὐτόνομος describes "cités et tribus qui au moment donné indépendantes, pourtant restaient dans la sphère d'influence d'autre puissance,"[50] but also that it (1) is not necessarily thought of as explicitly conferred or conceded by a superior power, and (2) cannot be reconciled with dominion (ἀρχή) exercized by a superior power. The same meaning underlies Thucydides' distinction between those Sicels who were subject (ὑπήκοοι) to Syracuse and those who dwelled in the interior and were αὐτόνομοι: the former had, by and large, not revolted from Syracuse when the Athenians arrived in Sicily in 415/14 B.C., while the latter gave their immediate support to the Athenians.[51] The opposition between ὑπήκοοι and αὐτόνομοι is practically identical with that between αὐτονομία and living under the ἀρχή of another power.

Two Thucydidean passages give the αὐτονομία of a small unit a modified sense which brings it close to the slightly pejorative use which we encountered in the *Antigone*. In his last speech, Pericles condemns those ἀπράγμονες who are willing to abandon the empire on the grounds that they would ruin not merely the state but also any enclave that they might be given to inhabit autonomously.[52] The αὐτονομία of these ἀπράγμονες, conceived as conceded to them by the state, is treated as every bit as asocial as Antigone's defiance of Creon's νόμοι, and the use of the adjective emphasizes their isolation from the rest of the patriotic citizenry. In the second passage the verb appears to describe the partisan designs of the oligarchs in 411 B.C. They had invited the Peloponnesian fleet to support them in their desire to keep the control of Athens and of her empire in oligarchical hands; failing this, to regain autonomy (αὐτονομεῖσθαι), presumably under an oligarchical government, with ships and walls intact; or, as a final possibility, to make any deal, including occupation by the enemy, to save their own skins from enraged democrats.[53] A comparison of these three options shows that αὐτονομεῖσθαι is less desirable than the exercise of imperial rule, but more desirable than foreign occupation with walls razed and fleet surrendered. It entails, therefore, the retention of walls and fleet intact, but spells the end of rule over the allies; conversely, it means that a city which exercises imperial rule over others is not said αὐτονομεῖσθαι. This implies that αὐτονομία involves only a minimum of independent sovereignty, an independence maintained by the approval of a foreign power rather than by the support of a state's own citizens. When and under what circumstances did this peculiar relationship come to be conceptualized?

III

We stated above that the peculiar use of αὐτόνομος in Sophocles' *Antigone* suggests that the concept was coined earlier than 441 B.C. How much earlier? Since the *Antigone* passage is our earliest witness for the concept, the only criteria for answering this question are circumstantial. We must find historical conditions which necessitated or made desirable the coining of αὐτονομία as a new concept in inter-state relations. If we make the reasonable assumption that their political independence was taken for granted by the Greek cities, large and small, κατὰ τὰ πάτρια and from time immemorial, we must conclude that the contingent independence expressed by αὐτονομία was not conceptualized until the independence of some states came to be challenged. Although such a challenge may have been involved in the synoecism of Attica,[54] it is unlikely that it created the concept, since the νομος-compounds did not assume a political meaning before the end of the sixth century,[55] and since Thucydides himself sees traces of the ancient autonomy of the Attic settlements as surviving into the early years of the Peloponnesian War:[56] his description of these settlements as αὐτονόμῳ οἰκήσει is, therefore, better interpreted as the use of fifth-century vocabulary to explain a situation prevailing in the hoary past. Similarly, it is improbable that the concept αὐτονομία was coined to describe the kind of socio-political situation prevailing in fifth-century Thrace settled for the most part by small autonomous tribal units rather than by city-states, units which are described as αὐτόνομοι in relation to the Odrysian kingdom which, it seems, could have threatened but did not in fact threaten their independence.[57] We must, rather, look for a period after the end of the sixth century, when the political connotation of νομος-compounds began to come to the fore, and especially to the time during and after the Persian Wars, when the autonomy of the Greek states was threatened first by Persia and then by the encroachments on independence by the Delian and Peloponnesian Leagues.

The earliest fifth-century incident in which αὐτονομία plays a part is in Herodotus' report of Xerxes' peace offer to the Athenians, transmitted after the battle of Salamis by Alexander of Macedon acting as Mardonius' agent. In return for withdrawing from the war, Xerxes promised to give the Athenians back their land and any further territory that they might wish to have, ἐόντες αὐτόνομοι, and to rebuild all the temples burnt by the Persians.[58] We are here obviously not dealing with the "descriptive" kind of autonomy, but with that which is conceded by a major to a minor power and involves the guarantee of its territorial integrity.[59] The concession and guarantee are in the present instance an invitation to treason, because they are given at a time when Persian troops were still in Thessaly, so that acceptance of Xerxes' terms would have been tantamount to capitulation. Accordingly, Mardonius' exhortation, ἔστε ἐλεύθεροι, ἡμῖν ὁμαιχμίην συνθέμενοι ἄνευ τε δόλου καὶ ἀπάτης,[60] has a very hollow ring and begs the question whether it is possible to be ἐλεύθεροι when the status of being αὐτόνομοι depends so completely on the sufferance of a superior power. It is, therefore, not surprising that the Athenian reply makes no reference to αὐτονομία at all and, in promising ἀλλ' ὅμως ἐλευθερίης γλιχόμενοι ἀμυνεύμεθα οὕτως ὅκως ἂν καί δυνώμεθα,[61] gives a different interpretation to ἐλευθερίη than had been implied in Mardonius' words, and at the same time sharply differentiates it from αὐτονομία: ἐλευθερίη is, in this context at least, something won by one's own efforts, while αὐτονομία is little more than a promise of noninterference in the internal and territorial affairs of a city given by an external power. Ἐλευθερίη, here, as elsewhere in Herodotus, is something worth fighting for, something which a state can proudly write on its banner;[62] αὐτονομία is either a purely descriptive term, as it is in the preface to the Deioces story at 1.96.1, or, as here, a status which depends on the whim and goodwill of a superior power. In short, if any inference can be drawn from this Herodotean passage, which constitutes our only evidence for the question of αὐτονομία during the Persian Wars, we cannot say that the Greek states felt their autonomy challenged by the Persians; what they did feel to be imperilled and what they did try to maintain against the Persian onslaught was something larger than αὐτονομία, to wit, ἐλευθερία which makes the independence of a state something won and maintained through its own efforts. The complexities which the concept of αὐτονομία thus displays in this passage make it unlikely that it was born of the confrontation of the Greeks with the Persians. As in the case of Thucydides' description of the Attic settlements before the synoecism, it is more probable that Herodotus retrojected into the past a concept which, though part and parcel of the usage of the later fifth century, did not play a part in the Persian Wars.[63]

There is a further association of αὐτονομία with the Persian Wars. In their speech to the Spartan judges in 429 B.C., the Plataeans claim that after the liberation of Greece (ἐλευθερώσας τὴν Ἑλλάδα) fifty years earlier, Pausanias "restored to the Plataeans their land and their city to settle it as their own autonomous possession; no one was ever to lead an army against them unjustly or to enslave them, and if anyone did, the allies present would defend her to the best of their power."[64] A proper understanding of this passage must take account not only (a) of the qualities here attributed to αὐτονόμους, but also of the double-barrelled historical questions: (b) is Pausanias' promise correctly represented by the Plataeans in the sense that we can infer that αὐτονομία was explicitly restored to them in 479 B.C.?; and (c) on the assumption that Thucydides here records the ξύμπασα γνώμη τῶν ἀληθῶς λεχθέντων (1.22.1), what was the purpose of the

Plataean allegation in 429 B.C. that Pausanias had promised them their αὐτονομία in 479 B.C.? Of these the second, (b), is of special interest to us, because it may yield some information on the role αὐτονομία may have played in the relations among the victorious Greek states after the end of the Persian Wars.

To begin with (a) the qualities here attributed to αὐτονομία. We immediately recognize a number of familiar features: it is again a status conceded by a major to a lesser power, by Pausanias, speaking on behalf of Sparta and of the Greek alliance, to the Plataeans.[65] Moreover, here as elsewhere αὐτονομία guarantees the territorial and political integrity of the state to which it is extended,[66] but it goes beyond a mere guarantee in that it binds not only the Spartans but all allies to come to the defence of Plataea if she should be attacked. Further, as in Xerxes' offer to Athens, being αὐτόνομος is related to being free, but the relation is slightly different here. With the use of the expression ἐλευθερίης γλιχόμενοι the Athenians had emphasized that freedom is something to be won by one's own efforts; the Plataeans, on the other hand, had already participated in the battle fought on their terrain[67] and are, therefore, included among the "Greeks who were willing to shoulder the risk of battle" when Pausanias had liberated Greece from the Persians.[68] In short, the freedom won for Greece (ἐλευθερώσας τὴν Ἑλλάδα) with the help of Plataea is the setting within which Pausanias declared the Plataeans αὐτονόμους in Sparta's name and in the name of the Hellenic League which participated in the battle.[69]

From a substantive point of view, the commitment by Pausanias and the Hellenic League was no doubt part of the treaty of Plataea of 479 B.C., aimed at transforming the alliance against Persia into a permanent organization.[70] Our main source for the terms of this treaty, Plutarch, attributes its formulation to Aristeides. The relevant clause declares the Plataeans to be "inviolable and sacrosanct in their capacity as sacrificers to the god--surely, to Zeus the Liberator, mentioned by Thucydides--in behalf of Greece."[71] Plutarch's paraphrase is, unfortunately, the fullest account of the terms of the treaty that has come down to us.[72] But it is full enough to leave no doubt that the protection of Plataea formed an important part of the treaty, and that this guarantee was confirmed by an oath is reliably attested by Thucydides.[73] Plataea's inviolability was thus a purely religious matter, related to the annual commemorative assembly to be held there and the penteric celebration of the Eleutheria, occasions prominently mentioned also in the Plataean appeal recorded by Thucydides (2.71.2).[74]

But in view of the geographical and political relationship between Plataea and Thebes, the guarantee will have had strong political implications. The long-standing enmity between these two cities had made Plataea a steadfast Athenian ally from 519 B.C. on,[75] her only ally in the battle of Marathon and, with Thespiae, the only Boeotian city to fight on the Greek side against the Persians.[76] Thebes, on the other hand, had joined the Persians after Thermopylae[77] and had fought against the Greeks at Plataea more enthusiastically than any other Greek state had done.[78] For that reason, she became the target of panhellenic vengefulness after Plataea: the Greeks marched against Thebes, besieged it, demanded the surrender of her leaders, and put them to death, perhaps on the basis of some version of the "Oath of Plataea," which was believed in the fourth century to have been sworn by the Greeks before the battle in 479 B.C.[79] Moreover, since the preserved "Oath" also singled out Plataea, in that only she, Athens, and Sparta are named by the allied states who promise not to lay waste each others' territory, starve each other into submission, or cut off one anothers' water supply,[80] it is possible that the Covenant extended to Plataea a guarantee not only of her right to administer the new cult of Zeus Eleutherios, but also of her territorial and political integrity against any future encroachments on the part of Thebes.[81] Such a guarantee can also be inferred from the language in which Thucydides makes the Plataeans describe the assurances of 479 B.C. fifty years later to the Peloponnesians,[82] and it is corroborated by the reply of Archidamus.[83] In both cases, the guarantee of political and territorial integrity is expressed by the αὐτονομ-stem; the Plataeans use αὐτονόμους, while Archidamus uses αὐτονομεῖσθε.

The problem of αὐτονομία was very much in the air in the 430s and 420s. The question, therefore, arises (b) whether the language of the Plataeans and of Archidamus is the actual language of the treaty of 479 B.C., or whether it is an interpretation of the guarantee of 479 B.C. in terms which had gained currency only after the treaty had been concluded, but were common enough by the last third of the fifth century. In other words, can we infer the existence of a concept of αὐτονομία in 479 B.C. from the language they used fifty years later?

An answer to this question has to take into consideration the use which, according to Thucydides, the Plataeans and their Spartan and Theban opponents in the early 420s made of the treaty of 479 B.C. Siewert recognizes in Thucydides' accounts terms of the treaty which are not included in Plutarch's paraphrase. He believes that in return for a guarantee of independence the Plataeans promised (1) to remain neutral, (2) to help in the liberation of the Greeks, and (3) not to enslave other members of the alliance.[84] But it is legitimate to doubt that Plataea explicitly gave any of these promises in 479 B.C.; rather, it looks as if these had been extrapolated by the Spartans and Thebans from general provisions of the treaty in order to justify the harsh treatment to be meted out to the Plataeans.

(1) We learn from Thucydides that several attempts were made by the Peloponnesians to elicit from the Plataeans a promise of neutrality in return for lifting the siege of their city in 429 B.C.;[85] but a Plataean promise of neutrality is assigned to the treaty of 479 B.C. in Thucydides' report only of the thinking of the Spartan judges sent to arbitrate between Thebes and Plataea in 427 B.C.[86] Between what powers can Plataea have been expected to be neutral in 479 B.C.? Surely not between the Greeks and Persians. Could they have been asked for a special undertaking to remain neutral in wars that might henceforth arise between two Greek states? A promise of that sort may indeed be read into the commitment made by all Greek states participating in the foundation of the Hellenic League in 481 B.C. not to go to war against one one another;[87] but even if we believe that it was included in the renewal of the alliance by the nonmedising states in 479 B.C.,[88] it is difficult to see why Plataea should have been singled out to give a special pledge of neutrality at that time. It seems much more likely that the "neutrality" of Plataea refers to neutrality between the two superpowers Athens and Sparta--or more precisely: the Delian and the Peloponnesian Leagues--to which it actually refers in those Thucydidean passages in which it is not related to the treaty of 479 B.C.[89] The opposition between these two powerblocks, and thus the problem of neutrality between them, was not yet on the horizon in 479 B.C., but it was very much the issue immediately before and after the outbreak of the Peloponnesian War. Moreover, it would have salved admirably the conscience of the Spartan judges of 427 B.C. to present the rejection of a policy of neutrality on the part of the Plataeans as a breach of a solemn commitment made to the Spartans on an earlier occasion. Accordingly, either the pledge to refrain from hostile action against other Greek states, renewed in 479 B.C., or the guarantee of inviolability given to Plataea in the treaty of 479 B.C., could have been interpreted by the Spartans in 427 B.C. as constituting a

pledge of Plataean neutrality, even though an explicit pledge to
that effect could not have been given in 479 B.C.

(2) Similarly, the Plataean promise to participate in the
liberation of the Greeks[90] was nothing peculiar to the Plataeans,
but can have been extrapolated from the common Greek undertaking
in 479 B.C. to levy troops to continue the war against the barbarians.[91] In this connection it is significant that, together with
the affirmation of Plataean autonomy, it is mentioned by Archidamus
in 429 B.C., when he tried to drive a wedge between the Plataeans
and the Athenians by inviting the former to participate in the
Peloponnesian crusade of liberating the Greeks from Athenian domination or else to remain neutral. There is no need to assume that
Plataea was bound by a special oath in return for assurances given
her.

(3) The same is true of the alleged Plataean promise in 479
B.C. not to enslave another member of the alliance. This statement
is made by the Thebans in their speech against the Plataeans before
the Spartan judges, and it is made with intent to undermine the
Plataean claim on the sympathy of the Spartans because of the role
they played in the Persian Wars.[92] The Thebans attribute Plataean
zeal during the Persian Wars to an excessive love of Athens combined with an equally intense hatred of Thebes, and this love of
Athens, the Thebans assert, made the Plataeans violate the terms
of the alliance they had sworn to by joining the Athenians in "enslaving" the Aeginetans and other members of the alliance.[93] The
enslavement of a Greek state by another member state of the Hellenic League cannot have been an explicit clause in the treaty of
479 B.C., but it may have been extrapolated in 427 B.C. from a
clause resembling the pledge in the inscriptional version of the
Oath of Plataea not to overthrow Athens, Sparta, Plataea, or any
other allied state.[94] That the original version of the Oath made
explicit mention of Athens and Sparta is unlikely; that it singled
out Plataea, because of the new cult of Zeus the Liberator and because of past Theban hostility, is possible.[95] But while the reduction of Plataea--probably by Thebes--may have been a concern of
the Greeks in 479 B.C., the enslavement of a Greek state *by* Plataea, of which the Thebans speak in Thucydides, can hardly have
been envisaged by the Hellenic League at that time. The possible
"enslavement" of the Greeks to the Persians was an idea that had
come up before and especially during the Persian Wars;[96] but the
idea that one member state of a Greek alliance would enslave another
was the product of rising Athenian imperialism, beginning with the

reduction of Naxos in 468 B.C., and of the anti-Athenian sentiment and propaganda it evoked immediately before and after the outbreak of the Peloponnesian War.[97] It is this latter kind of "enslavement" which the Thebans retroject into the treaty of 479 B.C., in order to make the Plataean alliance with Athens overshadow the embarrassment they felt about their own policy fifty-two years earlier. Theirs is a propaganda statement, which cannot be used in the form in which it is presented to reconstruct the actual terms of the treaty of 479 B.C.

To sum up: the speeches as reported by Thucydides can only be used with extreme caution to reconstruct the provisions concerning Plataea in 479 B.C. The neutrality of Plataea is presented as something going on in the minds of the Spartan judges; Plataea's promise to participate in liberating the Greeks is put into the mouth of Archidamus to score a rhetorical point; and the promise not to enslave Greeks is adduced by the Thebans for a similar purpose. All this can have been extrapolated from what we know--from Herodotus, Plutarch, and what parts of the Oath seem authentic--of the general terms of the Hellenic League in 481 B.C. as made permanent in 479 B.C. What we get from the speeches in Thucydides is a biased version of the facts tailored by Spartans and Thebans to fit a situation which was in 429 and 427 B.C. not what it had been in 479 B.C.; they give us reliable information about views held on the Hellenic League in the early 420s, but they tell us little about the actualities of 479 B.C.[98]

This must make us wary of regarding the Plataeans' use of αὐτονόμους οἰκεῖν and Archidamus' use of αὐτονομεῖσθε[99] as authentic quotes from a document of 479 B.C., despite the fact that, in terms of what we have already learned about αὐτονομία, it would not have been an inappropriate term for describing the status guaranteed to Plataea in 479 B.C. Her independence had been a traditional fact from time immemorial (κατὰ τὰ πάτρια);[100] it was in 479 B.C. conceded by a major power--the Hellenic League--to a minor power to ensure its political and territorial integrity;[101] it cannot be reconciled with domination by an external power, in this case Thebes;[102] and it is described by the Plataeans in Thucydides as differing from ἐλευθερία in that the liberation of Greece from Persia was a precondition for Pausanias' promise of Plataean autonomy.[103] Nevertheless, since, as we saw in our discussion of Mardonius' offer to the Athenians, the Greeks still thought at this time of the independence of their cities in terms of the ἐλευθερία which they had won from the Persians, it is not likely that the

city where the liberation was to be commemorated by the worship of
Zeus Eleutherios, should at the same time have been guaranteed a
status other than that of the full enjoyment of the ἐλευθερία
which she had won along with the other members of the Hellenic
League. The situation in Greece was not yet such that αὐτονομία
had to be coined to define a status different from ἐλευθερία.[104]

There is one further observation (c) which, in explaining why
αὐτονομία was a good term for the Plataeans to use in 429 B.C.,
makes it unlikely that it had been used to define the status of
Plataea in 479 B.C. It is noteworthy that the Plataeans do not
raise the point of their αὐτονομία in their argument with the Thebans, despite the fact that it would have been an excellent response to Theban complaints that Plataea had remained aloof from
the Boeotian League.[105] Their claim to the right αὐτονόμους οἰκεῖν
is only made in their speech to Archidamus in 429 B.C.[106] Why?
The plea is with the Spartans and is aimed at raising the siege of
Plataea and preventing the ravaging of her lands, a situation which
makes it singularly appropriate that the Plataeans should present
the guarantee of 479 B.C. as contracted by the Spartan Pausanias:
to proceed with the siege would be a violation of a promise given
by Sparta. Moreover, Plataea's appeal is made at a time when
Sparta's professed war aims included the restoration of αὐτονομία
to those Greeks whom Athens had enslaved.[107] The Plataean claim
αὐτονόμους οἰκεῖν thus becomes a test of the sincerity of Sparta's
professed purpose, more comprehensible as a diplomatic device in
429 B.C. than as a verbatim reference to the terms of the guarantee of 479 B.C. We cannot prove whether or not the αὐτονομ-stem
was used to define the status of Plataea in the treaty of 479 B.C.
Since these three passages in two Thucydidean speeches are our only
source, we cannot assume that it was so used, and there are cogent
historical arguments against it. For, as we have seen, Thucydides
is less interested in the antiquarian pursuit of preserving the
ipsissima verba or even the precise terms of the treaty of 479 B.C.
than he is in showing what use was made of its provisions in the
diplomacy of his own time. We can infer from Thucydides that
αὐτονομία was an important political concept in the early 420s; we
cannot infer that it had assumed that importance already fifty
years earlier.

IV

If we have succeeded in demonstrating that the αὐτονομία of
all Greek states--at least of all those which had joined the common

resistance to Persia--was taken for granted as late as 479 B.C., and that, therefore, the use of the αὐτονομ-stem in Herodotus and in the speeches of Thucydides cannot be taken as evidence for the existence of a concept of αὐτονομία at that time, we must regard 479 B.C. as a *terminus post quem* for its origin. A *terminus ante* is provided by Thucydides' report that part of the reason for convoking the first Lacedaemonian Congress in 432 B.C. was Aegina's complaint that she did not enjoy "the autonomy stipulated by the treaty."[108] That this is official language is corroborated by the demand Αἴγιναν αὐτόνομον ἀφιέναι which formed part of the Spartan ultimatum to Athens immediately before the war,[109] and the mention of "the treaty" enables us to push the lower limit of the development of αὐτονομία as a political concept back to the Thirty-Years' Peace of 446/5 B.C., which almost certainly is the treaty to which the Aeginetans refer.[110] This means that we have pushed the lower limit back to five years before the *Antigone*.

Between these two termini, the earliest historical event in connection with which αὐτονομία is mentioned is Thucydides' description of the relation between Athens and her allies at the founding of the Delian League in 477 B.C. Can we infer from his description: ἡγούμενοι δὲ αὐτονόμων τὸ πρῶτον τῶν ξυμμάχων καὶ ἀπὸ κοινῶν ξυνόδων βουλευόντων[111] that the concept αὐτονομία existed or was coined in the spring of 477 B.C.? The first observation to be made about this statement is that Thucydides predicates αὐτονομία only of the allies. Obviously this does not mean that the Athenians did not enjoy autonomy; it merely means, as it did in the alliance between Sparta and Argos of 418/17 B.C.,[112] that the autonomy of a major power could be taken for granted, whereas that of a minor power was not a matter of course at the time at which Thucydides wrote. Clearly αὐτονόμων here describes the status of minor powers as recognized by a major power, although in this context at least that status is not treated as conceded by as held.[113] Because Athens is the ἡγεμών, the question of her αὐτονομία does not even deserve mention. In the case of the weaker allies, on the other hand, the addition of αὐτονόμων helps to clarify their relation to Athens as envisaged in 477 B.C.

This raises the question whether the αὐτονομία of the allies received explicit mention either in the treaty or treaties by which the Delian League was founded or in the oaths which confirmed its foundation. The ancient sources are singularly unhelpful in answering this question; the context of the oaths is reported only tersely by Aristotle as τὸν αὐτὸν ἐχθρὸν εἶναι καὶ φίλον,[114] to which Plutarch adds that Aristeides administered the oaths to the Greeks and swore it on behalf of Athens,[115] and for the stipulations of the treaty we depend entirely on inferences from circumstantial statements in Thucydides and, to a lesser extent, other authors. From such statements it has been inferred, most recently by N.G.L. Hammond, that an "article of the foundation treaty concerned the autonomy of the members."[116] A closer examination of the circumstances which led to the foundation of the Delian League makes it, however, most unlikely that the αὐτονομία of the allies was the subject of an explicit guarantee in an original treaty. Thucydides presents the Delian League as initially no more than an outgrowth of the Hellenic League, involving no more than the transfer of leadership from Sparta to Athens.[117] Disenchantment with Pausanias' conduct at Byzantium and chagrin at Spartan reluctance to secure the independence of the Asiatic Greeks from Persia[118] prompted those Asiatic Greeks who had joined the Hellenic League *de facto* if not *de iure* after the battles of Plataea and Mycale to request the Athenians to take over the ἡγεμονία from the Spartans.[119] The request was for no more than a change in command;[120] the Hellenic League was not dissolved, even though not all its members, especially the Peloponnesians, acquiesced in the transfer of hegemony;[121] and the Athenians did not renounce their membership until after their dismissal from Ithome in 462/1 B.C., when they allied themselves with the erstwhile medizers Argos and Thessaly instead.[122] Since there had been no need in the Hellenic League to guarantee the autonomy of member states,[123] there is no reason why it should have been necessary under the new hegemony in 478/7 B.C.: under either leadership it could simply be taken for granted.[124] The allies were independent and only violence had ever prevented them from giving their allegiance to the ἡγεμών.[125]

From the beginning, Athens was the most powerful member of the League. Did the allies feel threatened by that in 477 B.C., so that they demanded a guarantee of their autonomy written into the founding instrument? What evidence we have suggests a negative answer. According to Thucydides, the request to the Athenians was initiated by the allies and motivated by an appeal to kinship;[126] Herodotus attributes the initiative to the Athenians themselves;[127] Aristotle has Aristeides inveigle the Ionians to abandon their alliance with the Lacedaemonians;[128] and Plutarch presents Aristeides as acting on the insistence of Chians, Samians, and Lesbians.[129] In a sense it is of little importance who took that first step, for regardless of whether Athenian imperialism was latent already at the founding of the Delian League,[130] or whether the Athenians were genuinely concerned for their Ionian kin, the self-interest of the Asiatic Greeks coincided in 478/7 B.C. with that of Athens to such a degree that they accepted Athenian leadership willingly.[131] Since there is no evidence that Sparta, as ἡγεμών, had ever threatened the autonomy of the member states of the Hellenic League, and since the only threat to the independence of the members of the Delian League could have come from Persia at that time, there is no reason why the allies should have suspected Athens in 478/7 B.C. of harboring imperialistic designs against them. Had they done so they would neither have invited the Athenians to assume leadership nor would they have acquiesced in it. Accordingly, it is inconceivable that they should have requested an explicit guarantee of their αὐτονομία included either in the treaty or in the oaths which marked the foundation of the Delian League. This means that Thucydides (1.97.1) states the mere fact of the autonomy of the allies in 478/7 B.C. not because he found it mentioned in a treaty, but because, as his subsequent account shows,[132] the later development from League (ξυμμαχία) into Empire (ἀρχή) makes it significant that initially (τὸ πρῶτον) there was no interference by Athens in the traditional autonomy of the allied states. Moreover, to make this point, Thucydides is constrained to use the language developed in reaction to such interference later in the history of the Delian League. His use of αὐτονόμων τῶν ξυμμάχων at 1.97.1 cannot, therefore, be taken as evidence for the existence of the concept of αὐτονομία in 477 B.C.

This gives us a new *terminus post quem* for the development of the concept. Between 477 and 446/5 B.C. there are two events in connection with which αὐτονομία is mentioned in the ancient sources, both in the years immediately preceding the Thirty-Years' Peace. The earlier of these is the Peace of Callias of 450/49 B.C., of which copies were certainly extant in the fourth century. According to two fourth-century sources, it guaranteed the αὐτονομία of the Greek cities in Asia Minor,[133] and this suggests that a phrase such as αὐτονόμους εἶναι τὰς κατὰ τὴν Ἀσίαν Ἑλληνίδας πόλεις appeared on the inscription which the fourth century knew and the authenticity of which Theopompus rejected.[134] Whether and, if so, to what extent this inscription depends on a fifth-century original is part of the unsolvable controversy whether a formal peace was or was not concluded between the Persians and the Athenians as representatives of the Delian League in 450/49 B.C. While I am strongly inclined to follow R. Meiggs in accepting a peace at this time as genuine,[135] even the coincidence of language used by Ephorus and Lycurgus is not sufficient to authenticate putative phrases from the original peace treaty. It is not impossible that in that treaty Persia recognized the Asiatic Greek cities as αὐτονόμους, especially if she still formally claimed the ἀρχαῖος δασμός from them;[136] but there is no conclusive evidence that a form of αὐτονομία was part of the language of a treaty in 450/49 B.C. At best the evidence of Ephorus and Lycurgus can be used to strengthen the likelihood that αὐτονομία was a recognized concept in interstate relations by that time. But whether it was must be established in a different way.

The second mention of αὐτονομία in connection with an event between our two *termini* is not any more helpful. We learn from Thucydides that after the Athenian defeat at Coronea in 447/6 B.C. the Boeotian exiles returned καὶ οἱ ἄλλοι πάντες αὐτόνομοι πάλιν ἐγένοντο.[137] The reference in πάλιν is of course to the state of affairs in Boeotia, before the battle of Oenophyta in 457/6 B.C. brought all its cities, with the exception of Thebes, under Athenian power:[138] when Athens lost her hold over Boeotia after Coronea, these cities regained their political independence within the framework of a Boeotian League under the leadership of Thebes.[139] We cannot know whether this passage is couched in the language used in 446/5 B.C. or whether, like the language put into the mouth of the Plataeans and of Archidamus, αὐτόνομοι retrojects into the past the vocabulary of the time at which this part of the pentekontaëteia was composed. Again, if we can find other evidence for the origin of the concept αὐτονομία, the present passage can be used only to strengthen an argument that αὐτονομία was familiar in the diplomatic language of 446/5 B.C., which we might expect a priori, anyway, since we have seen reason to believe that it did appear in the Thirty-Years' Peace a year later.

V

To find more positive indications when αὐτονομία may have entered the Greek language, we must start with the case of Aegina, the earliest in which we can be reasonably certain that it was used in a document: we recall that the Aeginetans alleged in 432/1 B.C. that they had lost the αὐτονομία guaranteed to them in the Thirty-Years' Peace. If we can discover (a) what curtailment of her independent status Aegina had experienced by 446/5 B.C. so as to necessitate its guarantee in a treaty between the superpowers Athens and Sparta, and (b) what further erosion, if any, had taken place between 446/5 and 432/1 B.C., we can be reasonably certain to have found at least some of the rights which constitute αὐτονομία. If we can then demonstrate that the treatment to which Aegina was subjected followed a pattern previously applied to other states, states, we may assume that other states who lost identical rights earlier can also be regarded as having lost their αὐτονομία, even when the term αὐτονομία is not explicitly used in defining this loss. We may further assume that the expression αὐτονομία was coined when the rights of which such states were being deprived first emerged as a recognizable pattern.

Concerning (b), deteriorations in relations between Athens and Aegina between the Thirty-Years' Peace and the outbreak of the Peloponnesian War, our sources are completely silent, although there must have been changes for the worse palpable enough to enable the Peloponnesians--with however little conviction--to make the failure to restore αὐτονομία to Aegina a *casus belli*.[140] We do, however, get some help to answer (a) from Thucydides' account of the conditions imposed upon Aegina when she surrendered to Athens in 457/6 B.C.: she had to raze her walls, surrender her fleet, and pay tribute, i.e., become a member of the Delian League.[141] Can this be construed as loss of αὐτονομία? Or, differently expressed, are any or all of possession of walls and of a fleet and freedom from tribute a precondition of αὐτονομία?

As far as the possession of walls and of a fleet is concerned, the evidence is conflicting. A number of passages suggest that the loss of walls and surrender of a fleet deprive a city of its αὐτονομία. For example, in the deliberations of the Athenian oligarchs of 411 B.C., which we had occasion to discuss earlier, one of the results envisaged by the invitation to the Peloponnesian fleet was to retain the autonomy of Athens (αὐτονομεῖσθαι) under oligarchical auspices with fleet and walls intact, contrasted with a foreign occupation which would spell the loss of both.[142] Likewise, in the debate concerning the fate of Mytilene, the possession of a fleet and walls is one of the essential elements in Cleon's definition of the Mytileneans as αὐτόνομοι;[143] and a passage in Andocides' speech *On the Peace* suggests that αὐτονομία still implied in the early fourth century the protection of walls and the building, repairing, and possession of triremes.[144] On the other hand, however, is the case of Chios. The Chians demolished their walls at the bidding of Athens in 425 B.C., and yet Chios continued to be considered autonomous down to the time of her revolt in 412 B.C.[145] But it is clear that this was done as a show of loyalty to Athens, and the fact that Chios was judged capable of revolt shows that she was still in control of her own affairs. In short, the Chians were not compelled to do what they did as the Aeginetans were, and they were not forced to surrender their fleet. Still, there is a question how important the possession of a fleet was to make a state αὐτόνομος. While there is some evidence that states whose ships were permitted to participate in campaigns side by side with the Athenian navy were regarded as αὐτόνομοι in contrast to states which only paid tribute,[146] there is no rigid consistency in that usage: participation with her ships makes Methymna αὐτόνομος in one passage but ὑπήκοος in another,[147] demonstrating that the distinction was not formally made *de iure*.[148]

Similarly, there is no reason to believe that the obligation to pay tribute to a major power automatically deprived a state of its αὐτονομία, if that obligation resulted from a negotiated agreement. It is true that in the passages just cited, tribute-paying allies are differentiated as ὑπήκοοι from the αὐτόνομοι who supply ships;[149] but, as we have seen in our discussion of the Peace of Nicias, the provision that Delphi be αὐτοτελεῖς as well as αὐτόνομοι suggests that αὐτονομία may be compatible with the payment of tribute, and the same treaty guarantees the αὐτονομία of six Thracian cities, "provided that they continue to pay the tribute assessed at the time of Aristeides."[150] Moreover, since Thucydides attributes the assessment of money and ships, respectively, to that time at the foundation of the Delian League at which the allies were still autonomous,[151] the mere fact of having to contribute one or the other cannot be regarded as a determining factor in defining a given state as αὐτόνομος. However, it is clear from one passage, not contradicted anywhere else, that the forcible collection of tribute due could be regarded as constituting a violation of the αὐτονομία of a state: when the Eleans tried to enforce payment by Lepreum of a talent owed (annually?) to Olympian Zeus by ravaging their land before arbitration procedures could begin, the Spartans judged αὐτονόμους εἶναι Λεπρεάτας καὶ ἀδικεῖν Ἠλείους.[152] That a state subjected to violence (βία) on the part of a stronger power in the collection of tribute or in any other way does not enjoy αὐτονομία is suggested by three other passages,[153] and confirms that in itself the payment of tribute is compatible with αὐτονομία.

What conclusions can we draw from all this for the αὐτονομία of Aegina? By itself neither the razing of her walls, nor the loss of her fleet, nor the payment of tribute constitute a loss of αὐτονομία. But since there is no evidence for any state being called αὐτόνομος which was compelled (and not merely requested) to demolish its walls *and* surrender its fleet, and since the payment of tribute is compatible with αὐτονομία only if it is not exacted under compulsion (βίᾳ), we may conclude that a state is αὐτόνομος when it is left free to exercise on its own the most rudimentary powers necessary for its survival. In practice it means that it can make its own decisions, free from violent interference by a stronger state, about what is and what is not in the interest of its survival, and that it can dispose of the military means necessary to implement measures necessary to ensure its survival. This explains why the possession of a fleet is indispensable for the maintenance of the αὐτονομία of Chios, Lesbos, Samos, and Aegina, but--we may surmise--not for the political independence of Boeotia or Lepreum, or why Chios needs no walls to be αὐτόνομος, as long as she can exercise some basic control over her own fleet. It explains also why in one context Methymna's control over her own fleet makes her αὐτόνομος, while in another passage the weakness of that fleet vis-à-vis the Athenian navy makes her merely ὑπήκοος. Our analysis so far is compatible with our earlier suggestion that the νομος-suffix of the compound refers to νόμος as the source of norms, so that αὐτονομία comes close to a concept of "self-government" which is willing to accept subordination in some matters to the desires of a major power;[154] this, in turn, accounts for the strange fact that αὐτονομία is mentioned so rarely in judicial or legislative contexts.[155] Our view seems confirmed by a passage which, I believe, has not received the attention it deserves in past discussions of αὐτονομία. The Athenian ambassador Euphemus is presented by Thucydides as explaining at Camarina the inconsistency between the attitude of Athens toward Chalcis and toward the Chalcidian colony Leontini with the words: καὶ ὁ Χαλκιδεύς, ὃν ἀλόγως ἡμᾶς φησὶ δουλωσαμένους τοὺς ἐνθάδε ἐλευθεροῦν, ξύμφορος ἡμῖν ἀπαράσκευος ὢν καὶ χρήματα μόνον φέρων, τὰ δὲ ἐνθάδε καὶ Λεοντῖνοι καὶ οἱ ἄλλοι φίλοι ὅτι μάλιστα αὐτονομούμενοι.[156] The opposition of αὐτονομούμενοι and the payment of tribute is familiar to us;[157] but, despite its uniqueness, its opposition to ἀπαράσκευος seems to touch a much more essential quality of αὐτονομία. In all of its thirteen occurrences in Thucydides the adjective connotes a lack of military preparation, often accompanied by psychological overtones of "not being ready."[158] This suggests that the ability to prepare militarily and politically for the defense of its political integrity is one of the hallmarks of a state which is αὐτονομούμενος, and we find the same idea again when Cleon defines part of the autonomy of Mytilene as consisting in her ability to defend herself with her own triremes.[159]

VI

Although the case of Aegina seems well-suited to identify some of the essential elements in αὐτονομία, it is also a special case in that (a) she lost her independence as a result of war and not of revolt,[160] and (b) she may have been a member of the Peloponnesian League before her reduction by Athens in 457/6 B.C.[161] We must, therefore, raise the question whether the same and/or additional criteria of αὐτονομία can be inferred for the original members of the Delian League whose autonomy under Athenian leadership Thucydides attests,[162] even if, as we hope to have shown, the original founding instrument of the League is unlikely to have used an αὐτονομ-word to define their status. After that, we may be able to determine more precisely the loss of what rights by what allies and at what time may have led to the coining of the concept of αὐτονομία.

In one sense the answer is simple and emerges from the surface meaning of Thucydides 1.96-97.1: unlike Aegina, which was coerced into League membership, the initial allies voluntarily (ἑκόντων) accepted Athenian leadership,[163] including the assessment of ships and money, respectively, which the Athenians imposed as tribute.[164] Moreover, since we can assume that their walls were as intact as they would wish them to be, we may conclude that they enjoyed full αὐτονομία in their relation to Athens. That the αὐτονομία of Athens as the major power is taken for granted has already been stated.[165] Her special position as ἡγεμών is further expressed in that the treasurers of the League, the Hellenotamiai, were from the beginning elected by and from among the Athenians,[166] and it is implied in that we hear of no assessment of either ships or money being made for Athens.

But there is one further element mentioned by Thucydides, of which we hear nothing in the case of Aegina. Thucydides describes the leadership of Athens at the founding of the Delian League as being over αὐτονόμων τὸ πρῶτον τῶν ξυμμάχων καὶ ἀπὸ κοινῶν ξυνόδων βουλευόντων:[167] if we interpret the καὶ here as epexegetic, as is grammatically possible, the exercise of αὐτονομία by the allies will have consisted in the voice each had in the deliberations on policy undertaken in "common" meetings. But to whom were the meetings "common"? To all the members of the alliance including Athens or to the allies alone? In other words, was the Delian League founded as a bicameral structure in which the decisions taken by the allies, meeting presumably under an Athenian chairman,[168] could not be implemented without the subsequent ratification by the Athenian Council and Assembly,[169] or did the Athenians meet with the allies jointly to formulate the policy of the League in an assembly in which each ally, including Athens, had one vote?[170] Obviously, the answer to this question is not without significance for Thucydides' view of what constituted the αὐτονομία of Athens' allies in 477 B.C.

Thucydides' language is ambiguous and permits either interpretation.[171] The same is true of Diodorus' report of the only League meeting of which we are informed: when he tells us that ὁ μὲν 'Αριστείδης συνεβούλευε τοῖς συμμάχοις ἅπασι κοινὴν ἄγουσι σύνοδον ἀποδεῖξαι [τὴν] Δῆλον κοινὸν ταμιεῖον,[172] we cannot tell whether Aristeides spoke as chairman over a meeting of allies only or as an Athenian delegate to a conference in which all allies who had taken the oath of alliance, including Athens, were "common" participants.[173]

Help toward an understanding of the organization and development of the Delian League, including the question of allied αὐτονομία, has been sought from the speech which Thucydides attributes to the Mytileneans at Olympia in their attempt to win Spartan support for their planned revolt in 428 B.C.[174] This can be fruitfully done only with constant awareness of the pitfalls Thucydidean speeches present for the extraction of historical facts, which we observed already in the case of the Plataean speech before their Spartan judges. In the present instance, it is all too often forgotten that the purpose of the Mytileneans is not to enlighten the Spartans on obscure points of procedure in meetings of the Delian League, but to justify their past relation to Athens in such a way that their present plan to defect will not appear to the Spartans to be mere opportunism, so that the Spartans will not reject them as potentially unreliable allies. To present their past and present actions in a favorable light is a greater concern to them than to be historically accurate.[175]

Of interest here is the Mytilenean view of their own αὐτονομία, of the erstwhile αὐτονομία of the allied states in the Delian League, and of the relation of both to Athens. Three times the word αὐτόνομοι punctuates their speech, marking three stages in the development of their relations to Athens, in order to demonstrate to their Spartan listeners that Athenian acts were responsible for the deterioration of that relationship. The first, in which αὐτόνομοι is bracketed with ἐλεύθεροι, comes at the end of a passage which explains their initial reasons for joining the League and their incipient disappointment with Athenian policy: their alliance, the Mytileneans begin, was with the Greeks to liberate Greek states from the Persians; it was not with the Athenians to enslave the Greeks.[176] If this recognizes the special position of Athens as ἡγεμών, which Thucydides had already indicated in his own name at 1.96.1 and 97.1, the next sentence shows that that position was willingly accepted "as long as they exercised their leadership on a basis of equality."[177] The combination of the recognition of one's own political independence as contingent upon the sufferance of a stronger power with the equality conceded by the stronger power to its weaker partner enables us to take this sentence as an anticipation of the description the Mytileneans give of themselves as αὐτόνομοι καὶ ἐλεύθεροι τῷ ὀνόματι a few lines later, and it tallies well with their later assertion that, though the Athenians still treat them ἀπὸ τοῦ ἴσου, none of the allies has any real αὐτονομία.[178] In short, the Mytileneans declare that they willingly accepted Athenian leadership as long as Athens respected the military strength the allies were contributing to the common cause. Athens' abandonment of that cause, the Mytileneans continue, and the enslavement of the allies which took its place caused a change in the attitude of the allies in that they became apprehensive about what might be in store for them.[179]

The next two statements reveal their views of the subsequent course of the αὐτονομία of the allies. In order to forestall embarrassing Spartan questions: "Why, then, didn't you do anything about your fears?" and "Why did you continue to participate in Athenian campaigns, if their aim was only to reduce Greek states to slavery?", the Mytileneans allege first: ἀδύνατοι δὲ ὄντες καθ' ἓν γενόμενοι διὰ πολυψηφίαν ἀμύνασθαι οἱ ξύμμαχοι ἐδουλώθησαν πλὴν ἡμῶν καὶ Χίων, and second: ἡμεῖς δὲ αὐτόνομοι δὴ ὄντες καὶ ἐλεύθεροι τῷ ὀνόματι ξυνεστρατεύσαμεν.[180] In other words, the Mytileneans excuse first their own inaction against Athens and then their participation in the enslavement of allies by implicitly including themselves among the helpless allies and by arguing that their independence and freedom were more formal than real. By trying to subtract what is merely self-serving in their argument, we can extract the following historical facts about αὐτονομία from this text. In the first place, since voting presumably took place at the κοιναί ξύνοδοι of which we hear at 1.97.1, the πολυψηφία, said here to have constituted an obstacle to a united stand by the allies against Athens, suggests that (a) common meetings of the Delian League continued to be convened even after the Athenians had begun to enslave allies; (b) matters of League policy were still discussed and perhaps decided in these meetings; (c) if the League had been differently organized, its decisions might have compelled Athens to abandon her policy of enslavement, but in fact (d) so many states had the right to vote that Athens could always count on sufficient support to stifle opposition.[181] The passage provides some enlightenment on the problem of whether the Delian League was organized in a bicameral or unicameral fashion. For although obviously the outvoting of an opposition could have taken place at meetings attended by the allies alone as well as at meetings in which the Athenians participated on an equal footing, it is worth observing that if the League-organization had been bicameral, the Mytileneans would have had a much stronger argument on their side, if they had explained the ineffectiveness of allied resistance by saying that decisions taken by the allies in their κοιναί ξύνοδοι were always subject to an Athenian veto. This adds some circumstantial evidence to a belief in a unicameral organization, and confirms that the Athenians observed at least the formality of letting the allied members of the League participate in decision-making even after the League had become an Empire.[182] Is it possible that the right to participate in the κοιναί ξύνοδοι was a mark of αὐτονομία of participating members?[183] The Mytileneans suggest that it was not when they identify themselves and the Chians as the only αὐτόνομοι left, and we know nothing of meetings in which only the Chians, Mytileneans, and Athenians participated. But, on the other hand, are the Mytileneans telling the truth when they allege that the membership of autonomous states had shrunk so drastically by 428 B.C.? It is difficult to believe that, for example, the six states of the Thraceward District, whose αὐτονομία is restored by the Peace of Nicias, had not been autonomous before they seceded, most of them only in the mid-420s.[184] If we add to this the anomalous and sometimes inconsistent usages of αὐτόνομος in Thucydides' listing of Athenian allies on the Sicilian Expedition,[185] we can only conclude that, even if there was some kind of formal recognition of the αὐτονομία of a state, the description of a state as *de facto* αὐτόνομος was open to considerable subjective variations. This would suggest that we need not take the Mytileneans literally and that we may interpret them as saying no more than that they and the Chians, as the militarily and politically strongest member states of the Delian League after Athens, were not enslaved but that the αὐτονομία which this implied may have formally existed, but only as an empty shell which afforded no protection against possible Athenian designs.

The second occurrence of αὐτόνομοι in the Mytilenean speech corroborates the correctness of this interpretation. After saying that the Athenians forfeited their trust by subjugating those who, like the Mytileneans, had concluded a treaty with them,[186] they state that fears of Athenian intervention would be unfounded, εἰ μὲν αὐτόνομοι ἔτι ἦμεν ἅπαντες.[187] The presence of ἔτι indicates that there was a time when all the allies enjoyed αὐτονομία, and the contrary-to-fact construction underlines that the formal autonomy still enjoyed by the Chians and Mytileneans has no foundation in fact in that it is negated by the constant threat posed by Athenian aggressiveness. But despite that allegation the Mytileneans admit that their relation to Athens is still on a basis of equality (ἀπὸ τοῦ ἴσου).[188] The reason for that, as the Mytileneans present it, is given in the third and final passage in which αὐτόνομοι occurs: "we were left autonomous for no other reason than that it was evident to them that, in their quest for empire, they must seize control by plausible argument and by applying diplomacy rather than force."[189] The αὐτονομία of the Mytileneans was, in their eyes, nothing but window-dressing for Athens.

If this completes the Mytilenean account of the nature of their αὐτονομία and its lack of substance, the reason why the Athenians chose this kind of propaganda still remains to be explained: ἅμα μὲν γὰρ μαρτυρίῳ ἐχρῶντο μὴ ἂν τούς γε ἰσοψήφους ἄκοντας, εἰ μή τι ἠδίκουν οἷς ἐπῆσαν, ξυστρατεύειν· ἐν τῷ αὐτῷ δὲ καὶ τὰ κράτιστα ἐπί τε τοὺς ὑποδεεστέρους πρώτους ξυνεπῆγον καὶ τὰ τελευταῖα λιπόντες τοῦ ἄλλου περιῃρημένου ἀσθενέστερα ἔμελλον ἕξειν.[190] The second half of this sentence is of interest to us only in that it tends to corroborate the view that αὐτονομία implies military and political power. But the first half is curious in that the Mytileneans not only attest a desire for formal justification of their imperial designs on the part of the Athenians, but also intimate, as they did at 3.10.5, that League meetings still took place to deliberate about common policy, even after the League had already become an Athenian Empire, implying that formally at least the right to vote in League meetings was a sign of allied αὐτονομία. This much is clear, regardless of the meaning that lurks behind the controversial ἰσοψήφους. It is further clear that, according to the Athenian argument, to be ἰσόψηφος an ally will have been αὐτόνομος. This, in turn, makes it impossible for us to accept at its face value the earlier Mytilenean contention (3.10.5) that only they and the Chians were formally left αὐτόνομοι among the allies. For it is inconceivable (a) that the κοιναὶ ξύνοδοι of the League should have consisted of three member-states only, and (b) that if Mytilene and Chios were the only states left with a "vote equal" to that of Athens, they could not and would not easily have been able to take a common stand against Athens, since no πολυψηφία would have inhibited them. In other words, the Mytileneans are trying to confuse the Spartans by playing the formal status of an αὐτόνομος against its actual exercise. The only historical conclusion we can draw from their arguments is that formally all allies (with the possible exception of some unknown cases of official exclusion from the κοιναὶ ξύνοδοι) were αὐτόνομοι and had "the same <right to> vote" as the Athenians had in the League meetings,[191] but that Athens, either by virtue of her position as ἡγεμών or by clever manipulation of League sessions, made both the meetings and the αὐτονομία of all allies *de facto* nothing but an empty form. In the present speech, it is in the interest of the Mytileneans to single out themselves and the Chians as the only possessors of αὐτονομία, because their power and special position vis-à-vis Athens were more visible in the Greek world than that of the lesser allies. They are intent on demonstrating that they are not αὐτόνομοι in fact only to justify their past failure to have opposed Athenian imperialism and their participation in the enslavement of the Greeks. Their speech proves historically merely that, according to Thucydides, αὐτονομία still formally existed in 428 B.C. but that it no longer mattered in the face of the dominant power of Athens.

The historical facts which can be extracted from the Mytilenean speech about the relation between Athens and her allies in the Delian League correspond fairly closely with what Thucydides had said in his own name in book 1. That the allies enjoyed αὐτονομία as long as Athens exercised her leadership on a basis of equality (ἀπὸ τοῦ ἴσου), and that the vote of Athens counted no more than that of each ally tallies with the statements of 1.96 and 97, where we learn that Athenian leadership was voluntarily accepted, that the allies were αὐτόνομοι, and that policy was made in common meetings between Athens and her allies. The Mytilenean point that the growth of Athenian power at the expense of the allies transformed allied αὐτονομία into an empty shell, useful only as window-dressing to conceal the imperial designs of Athens, corresponds to and is illuminated by 1.99, which, by describing the erosion of the initial "equality" of Athens and her allies, helps us understand in what that equality consisted.

The first point to observe is that the equality is conceived in terms of allied participation in the military campaigns of the Delian League: οὔτε ξυνεστράτευον ἀπὸ τοῦ ἴσου is explained as a result of the reluctance of the allies to contribute men and ships and a concomitant preference for contributing money, which led to weakening of their own military posture (ἀπαράσκευοι καὶ ἄπειροι) and to strengthening the power of Athens.[192] In other words, "equality" is not quantitatively predicated on the number of men and ships contributed or on the amount of tribute paid, but it refers to the willingness of the allied states to take risks, "equal" to those of Athens, commensurate with their military resources. The progressive unwillingness of the allies to involve themselves directly in League campaigns, not the size of their tribute, is alleged by Thucydides to have eroded the basis of equality with Athens on which the Delian League had been founded. This erosion weakened the allies and made them defenceless and vulnerable to Athenian reprisals in case they wanted to revolt. We remember from our discussion of Aegina that a modicum of military and political resources, sufficient to meet defence needs, is one of the essential attributes of αὐτονομία.[193] We may, therefore, suspect that the attrition of the ἀπὸ τοῦ ἴσου relationship may have had an adverse effect on the status of an allied state as αὐτόνομος.

We argued earlier that the question of αὐτονομία did not arise at the time when the Delian League was founded in 477 B.C.[194] because the possibility was not then envisaged that Athens might deprive an allied state of its traditional right to exist as an independent unit. We must, therefore, look to a period and events in which this right could no longer be taken for granted as first experiencing the need to conceptualize it as αὐτονομία. To identify it is not difficult: it must be the period described in Thucydides 1.99, in which we learn that the initial military and political equality of the allies with Athens had given way to Athenian domination over what eventually came to be called "subjects" (ὑπήκοοι) or "slaves" (δοῦλοι).[195] The recognition on the part of the allies that the military and political potential they had lost amounted to a loss of the most basic rights of self-determination will have made them lament the loss of their αὐτονομία. Who first coined the term we are not told; it is unlikely to have been the Athenians, but rather those who had seen the Athenian pressures described by Thucydides applied first to others and then to themselves, so that a pattern had emerged: "for the Athenians were meticulous in what they exacted, and the pressures they brought to bear were painful on those who were neither accustomed nor willing to endure hardships."[196] Two groups can be distinguished among those states who were deprived of their independence in this way. There were, in the first place, those described by Thucydides in 1.99.3, allies who, in their eagerness to convert contributions of men and ships to cash contributions, came to be so weakened militarily that they had no hope of ever opposing the designs of Athens. The bulk of these would easily be coerced by Athens to support her policies in League meetings, and their πολυψηφία will have prevented the allies from taking a united stand against Athenian designs, as the Mytileneans stated.[197] They may nominally have been αὐτόνομοι, but in fact not have had the strength to assert their αὐτονομία. No details are known about the composition of this group.

But we do know a little more about the second group, those allies who lost their independence as the result of resistance or armed opposition to Athens. According to Thucydides, Naxos was the first of these: Ναξίοις δὲ ἀποστᾶσι μετὰ ταῦτα ἐπολέμησαν καὶ πολιορκίᾳ παρεστήσαντο, πρώτη τε αὕτη πόλις ξυμμαχὶς παρὰ τὸ καθεστηκὸς ἐδουλώθη, ἔπειτα δὲ καὶ τῶν ἄλλων ὡς ἑκάστῃ ξυνέβη.[198] The revolt and siege of Naxos was preceded by the capture of Eion from the Persians under the leadership of Cimon, by the seizure of Scyros, and by the conquest of Carystus.[199] The first two of these events are likely to have had the full support of Athens' allies in the Delian League, and it is possible that Naxian ships participated in the campaigns. After all, although both places were important for the security of the Athenian grain route to the Black Sea, the Persians had been in possession of Eion and the Dolopian pirates of Scyros had been a menace to all seafaring in the Aegean. The expedition against Carystus, however, was a more dubious implementation of the purposes of the League. For although Carystus had submitted to the Persians in 490 B.C., and had contributed ships to the Persian fleet in 480 B.C., she had been prevailed upon after Salamis by Themistocles to contribute money to the Greek cause and had been subjected to a punitive raid,[200] and it may have

been all too transparent to the allies that only the security of
the Athenian grain supply stood to benefit from the campaign
against her: the fact that Thucydides mentions that "the rest of
the Euboeans" did not participate in this expedition may indicate
that none of the allies joined it.[201]

There are good reasons to believe that the capture of Eion,
which is securely dated in 476/5 B.C., preceded the conquest of
Scyros and Carystus by some seven or eight years, and that the
revolt of Naxos followed hard upon the reduction of Scyros and
Carystus, possibly in 468 or 467 B.C.[202] We are given no explanation for the revolt of Naxos, but the chronology of events and the
terms imposed at the conclusion of the expeditions permit some informed guesses. Thucydides uses the word ἠνδραπόδισαν to describe
the terms imposed on Eion and on Scyros; whatever the precise
meaning of the word, it is different from ἐδουλώθη, used to describe the settlement after Naxos, and refers to treatment commonly inflicted upon individuals rather than the community after a
war was over.[203] The enslavement of part of the population of
Eion will have been unexceptionable to most Greeks and was far
enough in the past not to have prompted Naxos to revolt. It may
have been different in the case of Scyros. The fact that this
expedition was more closely aligned with Athenian interests than
with those of the League, was exploited by Athens for purely local
patriotic motives,[204] and ended with the dispatch of Athenian
settlers to the island may have chagrined the Naxians, especially
if they regarded the Eastern Aegean as a more urgent and legitimate area of League activities. Carystus, following close upon
Scyros, will have exacerbated such feelings, and though we are not
told of any ἀνδραποδισμός of Carystians, the treaty which ended
hostilities will no doubt have coerced Carystus to become a
tribute-paying member of the Delian League,[205] perhaps the earliest case of League membership coerced by war. There is no reason
to believe that Carystus' control of her own internal affairs was
affected; but it is not inconceivable that those allies who refused (?) to participate in the campaign, including Naxos, may
have looked upon the forcible imposition of tribute on a Greek
state as an encroachment on rights which were soon to crystallize
into the concept of αὐτονομία.[206]

Whether Naxos' was the first attempt to defect from the
Delian League we know no more than we know the reasons for her
defection, but it is certain that she was the first allied state
which παρὰ τὸ καθεστηκὸς ἐδουλώθη.[207] Contrary to the enslavement

of the inhabitants of Eion and Scyros, the δουλεία of Naxos was political in nature. Of what it consisted in concrete terms we are not told, but it certainly will have spelled the end of her political independence. Thucydides' comment that this political annihilation was inflicted παρὰ τὸ καθεστηκός, in violation of established rules, has been interpreted by some scholars as evidence that the original charter of the Delian League explicitly guaranteed the autonomy of the signatories.[208] While this interpretation is grammatically possible, it is not inevitable. "Thucydides' phrase παρὰ τὸ καθεστηκός does not necessarily imply the breaking of a formal agreement, but a change of status which was not anticipated in 477,"[209] and we have seen above reason to believe that the αὐτονομία of no Greek state was threatened at that time.[210] Rather it was an "unprecedented" thing to do to deprive a Greek state, especially when it was a formal ally, not merely of what was later called αὐτονομία, but of its political identity. The shock of this, coming as it did so soon after Carystus, will have stimulated Greek thinking on how far Athens would be justified in going in dealing with her allies as well as with other Greeks, and it is this thinking that will have given birth to the concept of αὐτονομία.

This birth may not have been long in coming. If the chronology we have accepted for the events so far discussed is correct, the revolt of Thasos will have followed the revolt of Naxos by only two or three years.[211] It was provoked by Athenian designs on Thasian mines and trading posts on the Thracian coast facing the island, and it seems that the expedition which Cimon led against the island consisted of Athenians alone.[212] When Thasos was forced to surrender after valiantly resisting for almost three years, the conditions to which she had to agree included the razing of her wall, the surrender of her fleet, the immediate payment of reparations and the future payment of tribute, and the surrender of her mainland possessions, especially her mine.[213] What became of the mainland colonies, that is, whether they became independent or whether the Athenians took them under direct control, we do not know. Except for their loss and the payment of reparations, the identity of the conditions imposed on Thasos in 463/2 B.C. with those those imposed on Aegina in 457/6 B.C. is remarkable. Since we concluded earlier that the latter constituted Aegina's loss of αὐτονομία,[214] we may assume that the conditions imposed on Thasos, too, spelled the end of her αὐτονομία. Unlike Naxos, Thasos will have retained control over her internal administration, but was deprived of the means to conduct a foreign policy of her own.

By 446/5 B.C., the date of the Thirty-Years' Peace, the term αὐτονομία had been coined.[215] We have certain knowledge only of Thasos and of Aegina as having to agree before that date to a dismantling of their walls, the surrender of their fleets, and the future payment of tribute; after 446/5 B.C. the same terms were imposed also on Samos and on Mytilene, after their revolts had been crushed in 439 and 427 B.C., respectively.[216] Moreover, sandwiched between his accounts of the revolt of Naxos and of the battle of the Eurymedon and the revolt of Thasos, Thucydides has a chapter which indicates that the Athenians took harsh measures against considerably more defections, failures to meet assessed quotas, and refusals to participate in military campaigns than he includes in his account,[217] and it is likely that many smaller allied states had been compelled by Athens to demolish their walls and surrender their fleet before the same terms were imposed on Aegina, which had not been a League member, in 457/6 B.C., perhaps even before Thasos was subjected to this fate in 463/2 B.C. It is to the period between the fall of Naxos and the fall of Aegina that we must look for the origin of the concept αὐτονομία, because it was in this period that the Athenians, by depriving those dominated by them of certain basic political rights, established at the same time a pattern of these rights which could be conceptualized under the single name of αὐτονομία. The revolt of Thasos is the earliest defection from the Delian League which we know to have had strong Spartan support.[218] Since we have absolutely nothing else to go on, the possible reasons for Sparta's support--the first anti-Athenian measure she undertook since the end of the Persian Wars--may yield us some clue about the origin of the concept αὐτονομία.

The realities of her actions notwithstanding, one of the professed aims of Sparta's foreign policy had been from time immemorial the liberty and political independence of all Greek states. Spared from tyranny herself, she enjoyed the reputation of having freed other Greek states from their tyrants;[219] after the conquest of Lydia by the Persians, she had warned Cyrus not to destroy any Greek city;[220] in one sense the Spartans Sperthias and Boulis, in another sense the speech of the Spartan ex-king Demaratus, are used by Herodotus as symbols of the freedom for which the Greeks fought in the Persian Wars.[221] When the Peloponnesian War broke out, the sympathies of most people were, according to Thucydides, on Sparta's side, supporting her avowed war aim of "liberating Greece."[222] Before the war, it was Sparta who had appropriated the cause of the αὐτονομία of Aegina and even of all Greek states as her own;[223] during the war αὐτονομία and ἐλευθερία were the essence of Brasidas' promise to Acanthus,[224] and the αὐτονομία of the Peloponnesian states figured prominently in the treaty between Sparta and Argos of 418/17 B.C., which we discussed above.[225]

It is easy to treat these professions with the cynicism which they so richly deserve. But that does not mean that responsible Spartans did not sincerely believe that these were the ideals for which Sparta traditionally stood. Adherence to these ideals may have prompted them to promise support to Thasos in her revolt against Athens in 465 B.C., especially if the Athenian treatment of Carystus, Naxos, and some smaller states had convinced her that a pattern of Athenian policy had emerged which could not be tolerated in the Greek world. It was not the ἐλευθερία of the affected states that was in question, but a freedom of political and military action compatible with membership in a League which was the counterpart of the Peloponnesian League headed by Sparta herself. If the commitment to Thasos was kept secret from the Athenians,[226] this does not mean that it was kept secret from all Greeks, and it is possible, though far from probable, that either the Spartans, the Thasians, or some other Greeks sympathetic to the cause of self-government coined αὐτονομία as a propaganda term about this time, in order to identify the cause for which they claimed to be fighting and perhaps even to rally others to its support.

VII

Etymologically, αὐτονομία has nothing to do with walls and ships. If we have used the forced deprivation of these as symptomatic of the loss of αὐτονομία, we have done so only because they are the only concrete signs of αὐτονομία in our sources.[227] Walls and ships were the mainstays of the political independence and self-government of islanders and it was the αὐτονομία of islanders which most commonly fell victim to Athenian imperialism. This does not mean of course that in some recorded or unrecorded circumstances other features may not have been regarded as equally symptomatic of αὐτονομία as ships and walls. We do not know whether the presence of Athenian military and civil officials in allied states was thought of as adversely affecting their status as αὐτόνομοι,[228] we have little precise information on the effect of colonies and cleruchies,[229] of the taking of hostages, of loyalty oaths demanded of allied cities,[230] and of the jurisdiction which

Athens arrogated unto herself in many cases involving the allies.[231] All these factors, and others besides, could not help but diminish the independence and self-government of the member states. But we have no way of telling what combination or what intensity of factors marked the point at which αὐτονομία ended and ἀρχή began.

There is reason to believe that the point was not clear to the ancients, either. As we have seen, only control over one's own fleet and walls intact seem to be an unequivocal sign of αὐτονομία. But surely that does not mean that of the Athenian allies at the outbreak of the Peloponnesian War only the states enumerated at Thucydides 2.9.4 had their walls and fleet intact, and that all others had had their walls demolished and their ships transferred to Athens. Unsatisfactory though that list is, it is considerably longer than the list of two presented by the Mytileneans to Sparta at 3.10.5. We are clearly faced with different sets of criteria for what constitutes αὐτονομία, because, as we saw in our discussion of the Mytilenean argument, αὐτονομία is not a rigorous enough term to withstand subjective manipulation.

This does not mean that the parties contracting the Thirty-Years' Peace in 446/5 B.C. did not have some idea of what was meant by the αὐτονομία guaranteed to Aegina.[232] Nothing in Pericles' brilliant response to Spartan protestations about the autonomy of Aegina in 432 B.C. suggests that there is any misunderstanding between Athens and Sparta about the meaning of the term. However, what both parties seem to agree on is that αὐτονομία has no specific substantive meaning, that, in other words, it is merely useful as a political football in the game of fixing the blame for the war that is sure to break out onto the other side. This is shown by the Spartans in their third embassy to Athens, when they extend their original specific demand, Αἴγιναν αὐτόνομον ἀφιέναι, to the general and vague εἰ τοὺς Ἕλληνας αὐτονόμους ἀφεῖτε,[233] and by Pericles, when he answers τὰς δὲ πόλεις ὅτι αὐτονόμους ἀφήσομεν, εἰ καὶ αὐτονόμους ἔχοντες ἐσπεισάμεθα, καὶ ὅταν κἀκεῖνοι ταῖς ἑαυτῶν ἀποδῶσι πόλεσι μὴ σφίσι τοῖς Λακεδαιμονίοις ἐπιτηδείως αὐτονομεῖσθαι, ἀλλ' αὐτοῖς ἑκάστοις ὡς βούλονται.[234] By avoiding explicit mention of Aegina, by leaving open the question of which cities were autonomous in 446/5 B.C., and by claiming that αὐτονομία is as much of a problem in the Peloponnesian as it is in the Delian League, he brushes aside the entire issue of αὐτονομία as meaningless when it comes to dealings between two power blocks.[235] The same kind of cynicism is also in evidence in another incident in 432 B.C., which illustrates that Pericles' estimate of Spartan views of αὐτονομία was not inaccurate. Plataean entreaties to Archidamus to respect their autonomy which, they allege, Pausanias guaranteed on behalf of all Greeks in 479 B.C.,[236] are answered by Archidamus: "in accordance with the guarantee given you by Pausanias, enjoy your autonomy and join us in liberating all those others who shared the risks at that time, who swore the same oaths you swore, and who are now under Athenian rule: it is for the sake of liberating them and the rest that the present war effort is being undertaken."[237] The Plataeans are free to exercise their independence, provided that they exercise it in the interest of the Peloponnesians.

Yet its insubstantial propaganda value notwithstanding, αὐτονομία can also be treated as a serious issue, as it is in the case of the Mytilenean revolt of 427 B.C. The complaint of the Mytileneans to the Spartans, which we have already discussed in order to determine the degree to which Athens' allies were and remained αὐτόνομοι in the Delian League,[238] also reflects a genuine desire on the part of the Mytileneans to be αὐτόνομοι not only "in name" but also in reality,[239] to be not merely a showpiece to cover the imperialistic campaigns of Athens.[240] The same serious tone is shown in Cleon's insistence that Mytilene's autonomy is real,[241] and in Diodotus' more profound insight that the revolt of Mytilene is that of "a free people which is held in subjection by violent means and naturally revolts to regain its autonomy."[242]

A sincere desire to give substance to αὐτονομία seems to underlie also Brasidas' promise to the people of Acanthus in 424 B.C., sincere to the extent that a soldier-diplomat can afford to be. While it is true that Thucydides would not have made him say to the Acanthians what he did, if he had not thought that, for better or for worse, the people of Acanthus would be most responsive to this kind of argument, it is also true that if any Spartan cherished a genuine belief in Sparta's professed aims of liberating the Greeks that man was Brasidas.[243] In fact, Brasidas opens his speech with the statement that he has come to lend truth to these war aims,[244] and then proceeds to tell his audience that he exacted an oath from the Lacedaemonian government to permit him to implement them in that ἦ μὴν οὓς ἂν ἔγωγε προσαγάγωμαι ξυμμάχους ἔσεσθαι αὐτονόμους, καὶ ἅμα οὐχ ἵνα ξυμμάχους ὑμᾶς ἔχωμεν ἢ βίᾳ ἢ ἀπάτῃ προσλαβόντες, ἀλλὰ τοὐναντίον ὑμῖν δεδουλωμένοις ὑπὸ Ἀθηναίων ξυμμαχήσοντες.[245] We do not know whether Acanthus was at this time regarded officially (τῷ ὀνόματι) by Athens as an αύτόνομος member of the League. If she was, Brasidas sets out to show her citizens that they are in fact "enslaved" to Athens and that alliance with Sparta would bring them real αύτονομία, provided that it is entered upon freely and not by that force or deceit which is irreconcilable with true αύτονομία. The fist begins to show beneath the velvet glove, and the glove is almost shed when Brasidas continues to explain that Sparta's overall aims are more important than that Acanthus should enter the alliance freely: ούδ' αὖ άρχῆς έφιέμεθα, παῦσαι δὲ μᾶλλον ἐτέρους σπεύδοντες τοὺς πλείους ἂν άδικοῖμεν, εἰ ξύμπασιν αύτονομίαν ἐπιφέροντες ὑμᾶς τοὺς ἐναντιουμένους περιίδοιμεν.[246] The touch of cynicism in these words does not make Brasidas' offer the less sincere: as a general he could hardly have been able to afford to withdraw, unless Acanthus voluntarily accepted the offered alliance. The Acanthians knew what was good for them. Moved both by his speech and by their own fear for their crops, they decided by secret vote to defect from Athens, but they made Brasidas affirm by oath their status as ξυμμάχους αύτονόμους before opening their city gates to his army.[247]

There are indications that αύτονομία was taken more seriously in the last quarter of the fifth century than it had been just before and immediately after the outbreak of the Peloponnesian War, and that attempts were made to define it more rigorously. That this turn was due to the appeal which Sparta's professed war aims had found in the Greek world is probable but not provable. Part of the evidence has already been discussed. It consists (a) in the guarantee of Delphi's independence in the Peace of Nicias, where the terms αύτοτελεῖς and αύτοδίκους are added to αύτονόμους, in order to differentiate her political and territorial integrity from self-determination in matters of taxation and from freedom of interference in her judiciary system, and where τὰ πάτρια are cited as the sanction of her independence;[248] (b) in the statement in the same treaty that payment of tribute to a major power is not incompatible with αύτονομία;[249] (c) in the association of αύτονομία with arbitration clauses in treaties actual and projected which, one might say, defines the independence of a state in terms of its willingness and ability to settle outstanding differences with another state without resorting to armed force rather than in terms of its military and political preparedness for self-defence;[250] and (d) in the addition of αύτοπόλιες to αύτόνομοι in the treaty between Sparta and Argos of 418/17 B.C., in order to admonish stronger cities not to attempt to extend their dominion over weaker states.[251] It seems to have played a part in the propaganda surrounding the Sicilian Expedition: in his speech at Camarina, Hermocrates contrasts the slavishness of the Ionians under the yoke of Athens with the freedom of the Dorians, whose settlement in Sicily ἀπ' αὐτονόμου τῆς Πελοποννήσου makes the point that ethnic bonds with the Peloponnese have left the Dorians in Sicily politically independent, whereas the Athenians try to dominate the Sicilian Ionians;[252] in his response the Athenian Euphemus argues that it is not kinship but the interest of Athens which decides whether a given state is to be left independent (αὐτονομούμενοι) or not;[253] and it is only in connection with the Sicilian Campaign that Thucydides differentiates, not always consistently,[254] the αὐτόνομοι from other categories of Athenian allies, mainly on the basis of supplying their own navy,[255] and makes the point that all the Dorians arrayed against them were αὐτόνομοι.[256]

The issue of αὐτονομία became important again within the Athenian Empire after the defeat in Sicily, which many of the allies took as a signal to defect. Therefore, when a revolt in Samos, supported by Athens, replaced an oligarchical with a democratic regime in 412 B.C., the Athenians restored to Samos the αὐτονομία of which they had deprived her after her unsuccessful secession in 439 B.C.[257] Gratitude for Samian loyalty went even further after the Athenian defeat at Aegospotami: a decree of 405 B.C. not only informs us that Athens granted all Samians Athenian citizenship,[258] but also makes a new contribution to the definition of αὐτονομία.[259] The grant of citizenship is followed by the words πολιτευομένος ὅπως ἂν αὐτοὶ βόλωνται (12-13), leaving the details to be worked out after the war (13-15). Then comes the sentence of special interest to us: τοῖς δὲ νόμοις χρῆσθαι τοῖς σφετέροις αὐτῶν αὐτόνομος ὄντας (15-16), followed by a confirmation of existing agreements (16-18). The sequence of clauses shows that αὐτόνομος is here not used to describe the political independence of Samos: that is done by the declaration that the Samians are free "to adopt a constitution of their choice"; the term is rather applied to judicial matters in that autonomy is described as the condition in which they can "use their own laws." Moreover, the fact that the existing agreements, including regulations on disputes arising between citizens of the two states,[260] form part of a separate clause shows that αὐτόνομος refers narrowly to the free use of the Samian lawcode at Samos. In other words, αὐτονομία here has neither the merely formal connotations which made it a political football in 432 B.C., nor does the νομος-suffix here refer to the source of

norms, as it did, for example, in the status given Delphi in 421
B.C., where it was differentiated from the right to raise and dispose of one's own revenues (αὐτοτελεῖς) and from freedom from external interference in judicial matters (αὐτόδικοι).[261] The referreference in νομος is simply to the statutes.[262]

One final incident remains to be discussed. In his account of the events immediately preceding the oligarchical coup of 411 B.C., Thucydides tells of the attempts by Athenian oligarchs to strengthen their hands by establishing oligarchies in as many allied states as possible. He describes in particular the unsuccessful efforts of Dieitrephes to win Thasos for the oligarchs: two months after he had established an oligarchy, the Thasians fortified their city with a wall and waited for the Spartans to come and give them their freedom from Athenian rule.[263] Thucydides concludes this account: περὶ μὲν οὖν τὴν Θάσον τἀναντία τοῖς τὴν ὀλιγαρχίαν καθιστᾶσι τῶν Ἀθηναίων ἐγένετο, δοκεῖν δέ μοι καὶ ἐν ἄλλοις πολλοῖς τῶν ὑπηκόων· σωφροσύνην γὰρ λαβοῦσαι αἱ πόλεις καὶ ἄδειαν τῶν πρασσομένων ἐχώρησαν ἐπὶ τὴν ἀντικρυς ἐλευθερίαν τῆς ἀπὸ τῶν Ἀθηναίων ὑπούλου αὐτονομίας οὐ προτιμήσαντες.[264] It is possible to infer from this passage that the method used by the Athenian oligarchs was to promise the various states αὐτονομία, which they helped along by overthrowing any democratic régime they encountered. That oligarchy was actually offered in the guise of αὐτονομία is supported by the epithet ὑπούλου, and its successful propaganda appeal shows that the subject states really wanted αὐτονομία, which is here tantamount to political self-determination. What the oligarchs did not expect was that, freed from the threat of Athenian retaliation as the allies now were, they preferred an ἐλευθερία, which gave them complete political independence, to an αὐτονομία, which would by definition recognize that their independence was contingent upon the good graces of a more powerful state.

VIII

This ends our account of the history of αὐτονομία in the Delian League. On the basis of Bickerman's conclusion that it describes a relationship between states, we have tried to differentiate it from other inter-state relations and to determine its meanings. We found reasons for believing that it was coined at the time at which the Delian League had begun to develop into an Athenian Empire, that is, in the period in which Naxos, Thasos, and other member states became restive under Athenian rule. It may well have originated as a protest by or on behalf of suppressed

allies insisting that Athens permit them to have the same right
consistent with membership in the Delian League to enjoy "their
own νόμοι" as Athens claimed for itself. But it is remarkable
that, with the single exception of the Samian decree of 405 B.C.,[265]
the νομος-suffix in αὐτονομία refers not to the legal or judiciary
system but to the potential of establishing one's own norms, primarily in political and military affairs. The hypothesis that the
concept came into being in opposition to a developing Athenian
Empire goes some way toward explaining an initially adverse attitude to it in Athens. It was acceptable to the Athenians when it
was to their advantage as, for example, in the Peace of Callias,
which may have guaranteed the autonomy of the Greek cities in Asia
Minor,[266] and in the Thirty-Years' Peace, in which the autonomy of
Aegina, though very probably included on Spartan insistence, was
unexpectedly favorable to Athens in that she did not have to surrender the island.[267] Still, its use in the *Antigone* and in
Pericles' last speech suggests that the Athenians did not greet it
with unalloyed enthusiasm,[268] and the cynical reception Pericles
gave to Spartan demands for the autonomy of Athens' allies betrays
the same negative sentiment.[269] But circumstances in the 420s
compelled Athens to change her attitude: if the revolt of Mytilene
and Brasidas' success at Acanthus contained any lesson, it was
that the drive for a genuine kind of αὐτονομία was very much alive
among the allies, and Diodotus at least recognized the need of
coping with it seriously and intelligently.[270] It continued to be
taken seriously by Athens for the remainder of the fifth century.
Euphemus' remark at Camarina that considerations of interest rather than kinship determine what allies Athens will leave αὐτονομούμενοι shows an awareness of the seriousness of the problem at a
time when Athens still had confidence in the strength of her
dominion.[271] But once she was defeated in Sicily, she came more
and more to the realization that empire in the sense in which she
had exercised it could not be maintained in the face of demands
for αὐτονομία on the part of those over whom it was exercised: the
Samians were granted autonomy immediately upon their revolt in 412
B.C.; in the same year, the Athenian oligarchs acted in the belief
that a promise of αὐτονομία would be one way to win support among
the allies; and when they saw the end of their régime approaching
a year later, they knew that the autonomy of Athens would spell
the end of her imperial rule.[272] The grant of autonomy to the
Selymbrians in 407 B.C. and the reconfirmation of Samian judicial
autonomy in 405 B.C. can perhaps be interpreted as the last

desperate attempts to hold on to what parts of the Empire she still could.[273]

A brief discussion of some features of the Second Athenian Confederacy of 377 B.C. will serve as a fitting epilogue, in that they reveal what Athens had learned from the mistakes she then recognized she had made in the Delian League.[274] While in the founding instrument of the Delian League, as we saw reason to believe, no reference was made to the αὐτονομία of the member states,[275] the Charter of the Second Athenian Confederacy not only guaranteed the autonomy of the allied states but defined its essential attributes in terms which clearly indicate that a repetition of past mistakes was deliberately to be avoided. The existence of an autonomy clause is attested by our only literary authority, Diodotus, in the words: πάσας δ' ὑπάρχειν αὐτονόμους, ἡγεμόσι χρωμένας 'Αθηναίοις,[276] but for its details we depend on the Decree of Aristoteles, sometimes called the "Charter of the Second Athenian Confederacy."[277] The preamble of the Charter proclaims as one of the purposes of the Confederacy the preservation of the "freedom and autonomy" of the Greeks from Spartan interference,[278] bracketing ἐλεύθερος with αὐτονόμος, perhaps, as Accame suggests, to combine the affirmation of sovereignty in international law with that of sovereignty in constitutional law,[279] or to extend the guarantee against Persian interference, given in the αὐτόνομος clause of the King's Peace of 387/6 B.C.[280] to possible Spartan designs on the ἐλευθερία of Greek states. The two terms are again bracketed in the invitation in the decree proper to Greeks and non-Greeks alike to join the Confederacy, and four conditions are enumerated to define the status of "free and autonomous": ...ἐξεῖναι αὐ[τ]ῶ[ι ἐλευθέρ]ωι ὄντι καὶ αὐτονόμωι, πολιτ[ευομέν]ωι πολιτείαν ἣν ἂν βόληται μήτε [φρορ]ὰν εἰσδεχομένωι μήτε ἄρχοντα ὑπο[δεχ]ομένωι μήτε φόρον φέροντι.[281] In other words, αὐτονομία explicitly precludes (a) the imposition by Athens of a--presumably democratic--form of government, enjoins her from establishing (b) military or (c) political control over an allied state by the dispatch of troops or of governors, and forbids her (d) to exact tribute. Furthermore, a clause not directly attached to the guarantee ἐλευθέρωι ὄντι καὶ αὐτονόμωι binds Athens and every Athenian citizen not to retain or acquire lands or houses in allied territories, evidently to forestall a fear on the part of the allies that the policy of establishing cleruchies might again become a means of imperial control.[282] It is possible to explain each of these conditions as dictated by the political situation in which Athens found herself in the Greek world, especially vis-à-vis Thebes and Sparta, in 378/7 B.C.[283] But it is also evident that the absence of such conditions from the Charter of the Delian League was held responsible in the early fourth century for the loss of αὐτονομία which the allies had experienced with the growth of Athenian domination over them in the fifth century.[284] Although none of these conditions appears explicitly as an attribute of αὐτονομία in the surviving writings of the fifth century, the very attempt to find a documentary definition of the concept in the Charter of the Second Athenian Confederacy constitutes an effort to prevent the perpetuation of past mistakes, not only in promising a better treatment to its allies, but also in seriously defining the minimum conditions of a concept which had never before been properly defined.

NOTES

[1] Thucydides 1.67.2, 139.1 and 3, 140.3, 144.2.

[2] E. J. Bickerman, "Autonomia: Sur un passage de Thucydide (1, 144, 2)," *Revue Internationale des Droits de l'Antiquité*[3] 5 (1958) 313-44. For a bibliography of earlier studies see pp. 324-25; for a more recent discussion, see W. Schuller, *Die Herrschaft der Athener im Ersten Attischen Seebund* (Berlin/New York, 1974) 109-11.

[3] Bickerman, "Autonomia," 327-32, 334-37, 343.

[4] Ibid., 339-41.

[5] To have the meaning which Bickerman (341) wants it to have, the adjective would have to be accented αὐτονόμος, since Greek verbal compounds in -ος whose first element is not a preposition are oxytone (or paroxytone, if ending in two short syllables) when their sense is active, and proparoxytone when their sense is passive; see Herodian in *Grammatici Graeci* 3.1.1 (Stuttgart, 1876) 234-35, accepted by Kühner-Gerth, *Ausführliche Grammatik der griechischen Sprache* 1.1³ (Hanover/Leipzig, 1890) 329; A. Debrunner, *Griechische Wortbildungslehre* (Heidelberg, 1917) 77-78; E. Risch, *Wortbildung der homerischen Sprache*² (Berlin/New York, 1974) 196-98; J. Vendryes, *Traité d'accentuation grecque* (Paris, 1904) 192-95; and Buck-Petersen, *A Reverse Index of Greek Nouns and Adjectives* (Chicago, 1945) 1.

[6] A possible exception is the Ὀλυμπιακὸς νόμος, on the basis of which the Eleans assessed a fine of 2,000 mnai against the Lacedaemonians for having attacked the fortress of Phyrkos and for having sent a hoplite force against Lepreon during an Olympic truce. The sanction by which enforcement could be attempted was to exclude the recalcitrant Spartans from the Olympic rites and games of 420 B.C. Apart from the fact that few states were in the position of Elis, i.e., able to use exclusion from panhellenic festivals as a stick, the weakness of this sanction is shown by the fear of Spartan use of force, against which a guard of young Eleans was posted, strengthened by contingents from Argos, Mantinea, and Athens; see Thucydides 5.49-50; cf. 5.31.2-5 and 34.1.

[7] This does not mean that τὰ πάτρια is not used in propaganda contexts. For example, when the Thebans complain repeatedly in Thucydides that the Plataeans had rejected τὰ πάτρια πάντων τῶν Βοιωτῶν (Thucydides 2.2.4; 3.61.2, 65.2, and 66.1), they evidently refer to the alliance of Boeotian states which had become some loose confederacy by 447 B.C., including the Plataeans despite their close relations with Athens and enmity toward Thebes; cf. J.A.O. Larsen, *Representative Government in Greek and Roman History* (Berkeley/Los Angeles, 1955) 31-40, and *Greek Federal States* (Oxford, 1968) 26-40, esp. 29 and 33-34. But since only the Thebans refer to the confederacy as τὰ πάτρια πάντων τῶν Βοιωτῶν and since neither the Peloponnesian League nor the Delian League ever seems to have appealed to their πάτρια, it is likely that the Theban expression has no official standing, but is only a propaganda device to create an unfavorable impression of the Plataeans.

[8] Thucydides 4.118.1, where the armistice guarantees access to Apollo's sanctuary and oracle at Delphi; and 5.18.2, where the peace grants access to all panhellenic sanctuaries. For the substantive

difference between the two clauses, see A. W. Gomme, *A Historical Commentary on Thucydides* (= *HCT*) 3 (Oxford, 1956) 596-97.

[9] Thucydides 4.118.3: περὶ δὲ τῶν χρημάτων τῶν τοῦ θεοῦ ἐπιμέλεσθαι ὅπως τοὺς ἀδικοῦντας ἐξευρήσομεν, ὀρθῶς καὶ δικαίως τοῖς πατρίοις νόμοις χρώμενοι καὶ ὑμεῖς καὶ ἡμεῖς καὶ τῶν ἄλλων οἱ βουλόμενοι, τοῖς πατρίοις νόμοις χρώμενοι πάντες. That some specific offense or set of offenses is here envisaged, and not a general rule, has rightly been stressed by Kirchhoff, Steup, and Gomme (see *HCT* 3.598).

[10] Thucydides 5.18.2: τὸ δ' ἱερὸν καὶ τὸν νεὼν τὸν ἐν Δελφοῖς τοῦ Ἀπόλλωνος καὶ Δελφοὺς αὐτονόμους εἶναι καὶ αὐτοτελεῖς καὶ αὐτοδίκους καὶ αὐτῶν καὶ τῆς γῆς τῆς ἑαυτῶν κατὰ τὰ πάτρια. For the meaning of αὐτονόμους in this phrase, see below, pp. 7-8.

[11] Idem, 4.118.8: "you shall submit to us and we to you in judicial proceedings according to traditional usage, settling disputes by judicial means without war."

[12] Idem, 4.122.4-5. For the details and a bibliography, see L. Piccirilli, *Gli arbitrati interstatali greci* 1 (Pisa, 1973) 121-23.

[13] Thucydides 1.78.4, 140.2, 144.2, 145; 7.18.2.

[14] On this point, see Gomme-Andrewes-Dover, *HCT* 4 (Oxford, 1970) 143 n. 1.

[15] So, e.g., V. Martin, *La vie internationale dans la Grèce des cités (VIe-IV^{e}s. av. J.-C.)* (Paris, 1940) 516-21.

[16] See F. Adcock and D. J. Moseley, *Diplomacy in Ancient Greece* (London, 1975) 210-11.

[17] Thucydides 5.18.4: ἢν δέ τι διάφορον ᾖ πρὸς ἀλλήλους, δικαίῳ χρήσθων καὶ ὅρκοις, καθ' ὅτι ἂν ξυνθῶνται.

[18] Idem, 5.77.5: "The cities in the Peloponnese, both small and large, shall be autonomous in the ancestral way."

[19] Idem, 5.77.7: ὅσσοι δ' ἐκτὸς Πελοποννάσω τῶν Λακεδαιμονίων ξύμμαχοί ἐντι, ἐν τῷ αὐτῷ ἐσσίονται ἐν τῷπερ καὶ τοὶ Λακεδαιμόνιοι, καὶ τοὶ τῶν Ἀργείων ξύμμαχοι ἐν τ<ῷ αὐτῷ ἐσσίονται ἐν τῷπερ καὶ τοὶ Ἀργεῖοι>, τὰν αὐτῶν ἔχοντες.

[20] Idem, 5.79.1: "submitting to judicial proceedings on fair and equal terms in the traditional way." A. Raeder (*L'arbitrage international chez les Hellènes* [= *Publications de l'Institut Nobel norvégien* 1] [Kristiania, 1912] 40-42) translates "et à des conditions égales et réciproques, ils se donnent les uns aux autres satisfaction par la voie judiciaire, comme aux temps des ancêtres." This is more of an interpretative paraphrase than a translation, for while the idea of reciprocity may well be implied in ἐπὶ τοῖς ἴσοις καὶ ὁμοίοις, the first member of the expression seems to refer to the fairness of the rules whereas the second refers to the impartial way in which the terms are to be applied; cf. L.-S.-J., s.v. ἴσος II.2, and the numerous passages cited there. Moreover, κατὰ τὰ πάτρια is not temporal.

[21] See Gomme-Andrewes-Dover, *HCT* 4.143, referring to 5.27.2 and 59.5.

²² Thucydides 5.79.1: "The other cities in the Peloponnese may participate in the treaty and the alliance, autonomous and each city by itself, controlling ots own territory as it traditionally has done, submitting to fair and impartial judicial proceedings." All modern texts print the comma which we have placed after καττὰ πάτρια before it, taking καττὰ πάτρια with the arbitration clause, as in the arbitration stipulated between Argos and Sparta. This is, however, objectionable on stylistic grounds, since κατά-expressions usually follow rather than precede stipulations. Thucydides 5.27.2 and 59.5 show that καττὰ πάτρια is not required with the phrase δίκας διδόντες τὰς ἴσας καὶ ὁμοίας.

²³ Idem, 5.27.2.

²⁴ Idem, 5.29.1, 33.1-3, 31.1-6 with Gomme-Andrewes-Dover, *HCT* 4.141.

²⁵ Thucydides 5.77.5 and 7.

²⁶ That the stipulation quoted at Thucydides 5.79.4 deals with relations among all allies, and not merely those from the Peloponnese (who were made to agree to arbitration procedure at 79.1) is not sufficiently recognized in the otherwise exemplary discussion of this clause in Gomme-Andrewes-Dover's note on 79.4. Dover's emendation: ...διακριθῆμεν <ἄδε>· αἰ [δέ] τις... (*HCT* 4.143-44) neatly solves the otherwise insoluble problem of διακριθῆμεν.

²⁷ Thucydides 5.79.4, where the phrase τὼς δὲ ἔτας καττὰ πάτρια δικάζεσθαι suggests that arrangements analogous to the Athenian δίκαι ἀπὸ συμβολῶν existed also both within and outside the Peloponnese, and that the procedures and cases covered by each particular treaty were sanctioned by a tradition recognized as valid by the present treaty.

²⁸ Thucydides 5.18.2: τὸ δ' ἱερὸν καὶ τὸν νεὼν τὸν ἐν Δελφοῖς τοῦ Ἀπόλλωνος καὶ Δελφοὺς αὐτονόμους εἶναι καὶ αὐτοτελεῖς καὶ αὐτοδίκους καὶ αὐτῶν καὶ τῆς γῆς τῆς ἑαυτῶν κατὰ τὰ πάτρια.

²⁹ Gomme, *HCT* 3.667.

³⁰ Thucydides 5.79.1, as discussed above, pp. 5-6.

³¹ Thucydides 5.27.2: ἥτις αὐτόνομός τέ ἐστι καὶ δίκας ἴσας καὶ ὁμοίας δίδωσι.

³² As Gomme-Andrewes-Dover (*HCT* 4.143) point out, the phrase is equivalent to δίκας τε διδόναι ὑμᾶς τε ἡμῖν καὶ ἡμᾶς ὑμῖν κατὰ τὰ πάτρια, τὰ ἀμφίλογα δίκῃ διαλύοντας ἄνευ πολέμου in the one-year armistice of 423 B.C.; see Thucydides 4.118.8 and n. 21 above.

³³ Thucydides 5.81 and 82.2.

³⁴ Idem, 5.18.5: τὰς δὲ πόλεις φερούσας τὸν φόρον τὸν ἐπ' Ἀριστείδου αὐτονόμους εἶναι, where the participle is presumably conditional, sc. "the cities shall be autonomous, provided that they pay the tribute assessed at the time of Aristeides." Gomme's view (*HCT* 3.669) that this is a guarantee against increase of the tribute in future is corroborated by the use of εἶναι rather than of ἀφεῖναι, which would have meant that these cities had not been αὐτόνομοι before but were now given their αὐτονομία.

³⁵ See above, n. 5, and M. Ostwald, *Nomos and the Beginnings of the Athenian Democracy* (Oxford, 1969) 26-29.

[36] Bickerman, "Autonomia," 339-41.

[37] The statistics for Thucydides are: αὐτόνομος, forty-one occurrences; αὐτονομία and αὐτονομέομαι, four each; apart from Thucydides, the adjective occurs once in Sophocles, twice in Herodotus, three times in the Hippocratic treatise *On Airs, Waters, Places*, and has been preserved in two inscriptions (*IG* i^3 66.11 and 127 [= R. Meiggs and D. Lewis, *A Selection of Greek Historical Inscriptions to the End of the Fifth Century B.C.* (Oxford, 1969) (= ML), no. 94] 16) and restored in one (*IG* i^3 118 [= ML, no. 87] 11).

[38] Sophocles, *Antigone* 817-22, esp. 821-22: "But living by your own laws (or perhaps: being a law unto yourself) you shall descend to Hades as no mortal ever has." As will become clear, I prefer Knox's reading (see n. 40 below) οὔκουν κλεινὴ καὶ ἔπαινον ἔχουσ'.... for line 817 to the οὐκοῦν adopted by all modern editors.

[39] Sir R. Jebb, *Sophocles: The Plays and Fragments*. Part III: *The Antigone*^{3} (Cambridge, 1900) on line 821 f.

[40] B.M.W. Knox, *The Heroic Temper* (Berkeley/Los Angeles, 1964) 66 with nn. 8 and 9.

[41] If the interpretation proposed above is correct, one might carry speculation one step further. If a note of deprecation can be sensed in the Chorus' description of Antigone as αὐτόνομος, that tone may well have been carried over into the metaphorical personal use from a political Athenian attitude toward those of her allies in the Delian League who were growing restive because they felt deprived of their αὐτονομία, a feeling upon which the Athenians can hardly have looked with approval. The revolt of Samos, against which his victory with the *Antigone* is said to have won Sophocles a generalship (see the *Argumentum* of Aristophanes of Byzantium), may well have been brewing at the time the play was first performed.

[42] [Hippocrates], *Aër.* 16.19 and 35; 23.37 (Jones).

[43] See especially ibid., 16.14-21 and 34-37: διὰ ταύτας ἐμοὶ δοκεῖ τὰς προφάσιας ἄναλκες εἶναι τὸ γένος τὸ Ἀσιηνὸν καὶ προσέτι διὰ τοὺς νόμους. τῆς γὰρ Ἀσίης τὰ πολλὰ βασιλεύεται. ὅκου δὲ μὴ αὐτοὶ ἑωυτῶν εἰσι καρτεροὶ οἱ ἄνθρωποι μηδὲ αὐτόνομοι, ἀλλὰ δεσπόζονται, οὐ περὶ τούτου αὐτοῖσιν ὁ λόγος ἐστίν, ὅκως τὰ πολέμια ἀσκήσωσιν, ἀλλ' ὅκως μὴ δόξωσι μάχιμοι εἶναι... ὁκόσοι γὰρ ἐν τῇ Ἀσίῃ Ἕλληνες ἢ βάρβαροι μὴ δεσπόζονται, ἀλλ' αὐτόνομοί εἰσι καὶ ἑωυτοῖσι ταλαιπωρεῦσιν, οὗτοι μαχιμώτατοί εἰσι πάντων.

[44] Ibid., 16.18: αὐτοὶ ἑωυτῶν εἰσι καρτεροί; 16.35-36 ἑωυτοῖσι ταλαιπωρεῦσιν; and 23.37-38: ὑπὲρ ἑωυτῶν γὰρ τοὺς κινδύνους αἱρεῦνται καὶ οὐκ ἄλλων.

[45] Thucydides 5.18.2 with pp. 7-8, above.

[46] Herodotus 1.96.1: After the fall of the Assyrian empire "all those on the mainland were autonomous, but fell again under one-man rule in the following manner."

[47] Thucydides 2.16.1: τῇ τε οὖν ἐπὶ πολὺ κατὰ τὴν χώραν αὐτονόμῳ οἰκήσει μετεῖχον οἱ Ἀθηναῖοι.

[48] Thucydides 2.29.2.

⁴⁹Thucydides 2.96.1-4: ἀνίστησιν οὖν ἐκ τῶν Ὀδρυσῶν ὁρμώμενος πρῶτον μὲν τούς... Θρᾷκας, ὅσων ἦρχε.... παρεκάλει δὲ καὶ τῶν ὀρεινῶν Θρᾳκῶν πολλοὺς τῶν αὐτονόμων καὶ μαχαιροφόρων... καὶ τοὺς μὲν μισθῷ ἔπειθεν, οἱ δ'ἐθελονταὶ ξυνηκολούθουν. ἀνίστη δὲ καὶ Ἀγριᾶνας καὶ Λαιαίους καὶ ἄλλα ὅσα ἔθνη Παιονικὰ ὧν ἦρχε.... ὡρίζετο ἡ ἀρχὴ τὰ πρὸς Παίονας αὐτονόμους ἤδη. τὰ δὲ πρὸς Τριβαλλούς, καὶ τούτους αὐτονόμους, Τρῆρες ὥριζον καὶ Τιλαταῖοι. Cf. also 98.3-4, where autonomous Thracians follow him ἀπαράκλητοι, and where the autonomous tribes from Rhodope are called the best fighters; and 101.3, where autonomous, sc. unsubjugated, tribes of the plain feared his attack.

⁵⁰Bickerman, "Autonomia," 328-32, esp. 328.

⁵¹Thucydides 6.88.4, where, with Gomme-Andrewes-Dover (*HCT* 4.360), I regard Canter's emendation of οἱ πολλοί to οὐ πολλοί as unavoidable.

⁵²Thucydides 2.63.3: τάχιστ' ἄν τε πόλιν οἱ τοιοῦτοι ἑτέρους τε πείσαντες ἀπολέσειαν καὶ εἴ που ἐπὶ σφῶν αὐτῶν αὐτόνομοι οἰκήσειαν.

⁵³Idem, 8.91.3: ἐκεῖνοι γὰρ μάλιστα μὲν ἐβούλοντο ὀλιγαρχούμενοι ἄρχειν καὶ τῶν ξυμμάχων, εἰ δὲ μή, τάς τε ναῦς καὶ τὰ τείχη ἔχοντες αὐτονομεῖσθαι, ἐξειργόμενοι δὲ καὶ τούτου μὴ οὖν ὑπὸ τοῦ δήμου γε αὖθις γενομένου αὐτοὶ πρὸ τῶν ἄλλων μάλιστα διαφθαρῆναι, ἀλλὰ καὶ τοὺς πολεμίους ἐσαγαγόμενοι ἄνευ τειχῶν καὶ νεῶν ξυμβῆναι καὶ ὁπωσοῦν τὰ τῆς πόλεως ἔχειν, εἰ τοῖς γε σώμασι σφῶν ἄδεια ἔσται.

⁵⁴See Thucydides' description at 2.15.1-2.

⁵⁵See Ostwald, *Nomos*, 157-58.

⁵⁶Thucydides 2.16.1-2.

⁵⁷Idem, 2.29.3, 96.2-4, 98.3-4, 101.3. It is not without significance that Thucydides does not apply the adjective, e.g., to the Aetolian communities.

⁵⁸Herodotus 8.140α.2: τοῦτο μὲν τὴν γῆν σφι ἀπόδος, τοῦτο δὲ ἄλλην πρὸς ταύτῃ ἑλέσθων αὐτοί, ἥντινα ἂν ἐθέλωσι, ἐόντες αὐτόνομοι. ἱρά τε πάντα σφι, ἢν δὴ βούλωνταί γε ἐμοὶ ὁμολογέειν, ἀνόρθωσον, ὅσα ἐγὼ ἐνέπρησα.

⁵⁹Cf. the guarantees given to Delphi in the Peace of Nicias at Thucydides 5.18.2, and by Sparta and Argos to the Peloponnesian cities (see 5.79.1; cf. 77.5). See above, pp. 4-6 and 7-8.

⁶⁰Herodotus 8.140α.4: "be free and make a compact of alliance with us without trickery and deceit."

⁶¹Idem, 8.143.1: "None the less, we stick by our freedom and will defend ourselves as best as we have power."

⁶²For the role of ἐλευθερίη in Herodotus, see K. von Fritz ("Die griechische ΕΛΕΥΘΕΡΙΑ bei Herodot," *Wiener Studien* 78 [1965] 5-31) who stresses the relation between ἐλευθερία and νόμος. It should be noted that Herodotus uses ἐλευθερίη, ἐλεύθερος, and ἐλευθερόω for the liberation of a state from internal despotism as well as for freedom from foreign domination. In addition to the present passage, the latter is described as worth preserving

or worth fighting for in the following passages: ἐλευθερίη at
2.102.4; 3.82.5; 4.133.2; 5.2.1; 6.5.1; 7.2.3; 9.98.3; ἐλεύθερος
at 1.210.2; 3.65.7, 125.3; 4.136.4, 139.2; 5.49.2, 64.2, 91.1,
109.2; 6.11.2, 109.3-6; 7.104.4, 139.5, 178.2; 9.45.2, 60.1;
ἐλευθερόω at 1.95.2, 127.1; 3.82.5; 4.137.1; 5.62.1-2, 63.1, 65.5,
78; 6.123.2; 7.157.2, 8.132.1, and 142.3. For a discussion of
ἐλευθερία and ἐλεύθερος as a rallying-cry in 480 B.C., see P.
Siewert, *Der Eid von Plataiai* (= *Vestigia* 16) (Munich, 1972) 53-56.

[63] Against this, it might be argued that Mardonius' offer to
Athens consists in the same status of αὐτονομία as the Greek cities
in Asia Minor enjoyed under Persian rule (cf. Bickerman, "Autonomia," 339-41) which the Athenians do not regard as good enough. I
believe my arguments against Bickerman (above, p. 10) to be sufficiently strong against that assumption.

[64] Thucydides 2.71.2: Παυσανίας γὰρ ὁ Κλεομβρότου Λακεδαιμό-
νιος ἐλευθερώσας τὴν Ἑλλάδα ἀπὸ τῶν Μήδων μετὰ Ἑλλήνων τῶν
ἐθελησάντων ξυνάρασθαι τὸν κίνδυνον τῆς μάχης ἣ παρ' ἡμῖν ἐγένετο,
θύσας ἐν τῇ Πλαταιῶν ἀγορᾷ ἱερὰ Διὶ ἐλευθερίῳ καὶ ξυγκαλέσας
πάντας τοὺς ξυμμάχους ἀπεδίδου Πλαταιεῦσι γῆν καὶ πόλιν τὴν σφετέραν ἔχοντας αὐτονόμους οἰκεῖν, στρατεῦσαί τε μηδένα ποτὲ ἀδίκως
ἐπ' αὐτοὺς μηδ' ἐπὶ δουλείᾳ· εἰ δὲ μή, ἀμύνειν τοὺς παρόντας
ξυμμάχους κατὰ δύναμιν. and 2.71.4: λέγομεν ὑμῖν γῆν τὴν Πλαταιίδα
μὴ ἀδικεῖν μηδὲ παραβαίνειν τοὺς ὅρκους, ἐᾶν δὲ οἰκεῖν αὐτονόμους
καθάπερ Παυσανίας ἐδικαίωσεν.

[65] There may even be a hint of the idea usually expressed by
κατὰ τὰ πάτρια in ἀπεδίδου, which Gomme rightly renders as "restored," "reinstated," rather than as "granted."

[66] Cf. Thucydides 5.18.2 and 5.79.1.

[67] Herodotus 9.28.6.

[68] See Thuc. 2.71.2 as quoted above, n. 64.

[69] This interpretation is confirmed by Archidamus' reply at
2.72.1: καθάπερ γὰρ Παυσανίας ὑμῖν παρέδωκεν, αὐτοί τε αὐτονομεῖσθε καὶ τοὺς ἄλλους ξυνελευθεροῦτε, ὅσοι μετασχόντες τῶν τότε
κινδύνων ὑμῖν τε ξυνώμοσαν.... We shall have to deal with some
peculiar aspects of this passage later; see below, p. 20.

[70] The existence of such a treaty was first posited by G.
Grote (*A History of Greece*, new ed. 4 [London, 1888] 282) and has
been argued in detail by J.A.O. Larsen ("The Constitution of the
Peloponnesian League," *CP* 28 [1933] 257-76, esp. 262-65; cf. also
HSCP 51 [1940] 176-80). Though doubted by a number of recent
scholars, it has been reaffirmed by R. Meiggs (*The Athenian Empire*
[Oxford, 1972] [= *AE*] 507-8) and P. Siewert (*Der Eid*, 89-93).

[71] Plutarch, *Aristeides* 21.1-2: Πλαταιεῖς δ' ἀσύλους καὶ
ἱεροὺς ἀφίεσθαι τῷ θεῷ θύοντας ὑπὲρ τῆς Ἑλλάδος.

[72] Modern scholars have seen additional terms reflected in the
accounts of Diodorus and of Thucydides; see, e.g., A. E. Raubitschek, "The Covenant of Plataea," *TAPA* 91 (1960) 178-83, esp. 181.
Siewert (*Der Eid*, 91) believes on the basis of Thucydides that (a)
the independence of Plataea was affirmed by an oath (2.71.2) and
that Plataea promised (b) to remain neutral (3.68.1), (c) to participate in the liberation of the Greeks (2.72.1), and (d) not to
enslave other members of the alliance (3.64.3). We shall deal
with these views critically below, pp. 18-21.

[73] Thucydides 3.59.2, 64.2; cf. 3.63.3 and 2.72.1.

[74] F. R. Wüst,("Amphiktyonie, Eidgenossenschaft, Symmachie," *Historia* 3 [1954-55] 129-53, esp. 144), in arguing that the Hellenic League was modelled on the Delphic Amphictyony, suggests that the new cult and festival were instituted as a deliberate parallel to institutions of that Amphictyony.

[75] Herodotus 6.108 with Thucydides 3.68.5.

[76] Herodotus 6.108.1 and 6; 7.132.1; 8.50.2, and ML, no. 27.6.

[77] For Theban policy up to Thermopylae, see Herodotus 7.132.1, 202, 205.2-3; Plutarch, *De Herodoti Malignitate*, *Moralia* 864e; after Thermopylae: Herodotus 8.66.2 and 9.2.

[78] Herodotus 9.40 and 67-68.

[79] Herodotus 9.86-88. For the text of the Oath, see M. N. Tod, *A Selection of Greek Historical Inscriptions* 2 (Oxford, 1948) no. 204.32-33; on the problem of authenticity, see Siewert, *Der Eid*, 75-97, esp. 81-83. That the section on the treatment of Thebes may be genuine is supported by two references in Xenophon (*Hellenica* 6.3.20 and 6.5.35) to the proverbial expression Θηβαίους δεκατευθῆναι; cf. also Polybius 9.39.5, Justin 11.3.10, and Aristodemus 104 F 3.4 (*FGH*).

[80] See Tod, *GHI* 2, no. 204.33-39.

[81] Even P. A. Brunt ("The Hellenic League against Persia," *Historia* 2 [1953-54] 135-63, esp. 153-54 and 157), who rejects Plutarch, *Aristeides* 21.1-2, as evidence for a general compact, believes that a covenant affecting Plataea alone was struck in 479 B.C.

[82] Thucydides 2.71.2: γῆν καὶ πόλιν τὴν σφετέραν ἔχοντας αὐτονόμους οἰκεῖν, στρατεῦσαί τε μηδένα ποτὲ ἀδίκως ἐπ' αὐτοὺς μηδ' ἐπὶ δουλείᾳ· εἰ δὲ μή, ἀμύνειν τοὺς παρόντας ξυμμάχους κατὰ δύναμιν. Cf. above, pp. 16-17 and n. 64.

[83] Thucydides 2.72.1.

[84] Idem, 3.68.1, 2.72.1, and 3.64.3 with Siewert, *Der Eid*, 91.

[85] Thucydides 2.72.1, 3.64.3, and 3.68.1. In the last of these passages, I refer to the words καὶ ὅτε ὕστερον [ἃ] πρὸ τοῦ περιτειχίζεσθαι προείχοντο αὐτοῖς, κοινοὺς εἶναι κατ' ἐκεῖνα.

[86] Idem, 3.68.1: τὸν τε ἄλλον χρόνον ἠξίουν δῆθεν αὐτοὺς κατὰ τὰς παλαιὰς Παυσανίου μετὰ τὸν Μῆδον σπονδὰς ἡσυχάζειν.

[87] Herodotus 7.145.1.

[88] See Siewert, *Der Eid*, 87-93.

[89] See n. 85 above.

[90] Thucydides 2.72.1.

[91] Plutarch, *Aristeides* 21.2.

[92] The Plataean arguments at Thucydides 3.54.3-5, 56.4-6, 57.2-4, 58.1 and 4-5, and 59.2, are countered by the Thebans at 63.2-3, 64.1-3, and 67.2.

[93] Thucydides 3.64.3: ἀπελίπετε γὰρ αὐτὴν <sc. τὴν τότε γενομένην ξυνωμοσίαν> καὶ παραβάντες ξυνκατεδουλοῦσθε μᾶλλον Αἰγινήτας καὶ ἄλλους τινὰς τῶν ξυνομοσάντων ἢ διεκωλύετε.

[94] Tod, *GHI* 2, no. 204.32-33, with Siewert, *Der Eid*, 81-97.

[95] Cf. Thucydides 2.71.2: στρατεῦσαί τε μηδένα ποτὲ ἀδίκως ἐπ' αὐτοὺς μηδ' ἐπὶ δουλείᾳ; Plutarch, *Aristeides* 21.2: Πλαταιεῖς δ' ἀσύλους καὶ ἱεροὺς ἀφίεσθαι τῷ θεῷ θύοντας ὑπὲρ τῆς Ἑλλάδος.

[96] ML, no. 26.I.4; Aeschylus, *Persae* 50, 242, 745; Herodotus 1.27.4, 164.2, 169.1-2, 170.2, 174.1; 4.93, 118.4; 5.49.2-3, 116; 6.11.2, 12.3, 32, 44.1, 45.1, 106.2, 109.3; 7.51.2, 102.2, 108.1, 235.3; 8.22.1, 100.3 and 5, 101.3, 142.3, 144.1; 9.45.2, 48.2, 60.1, 90.2; Thucydides 1.18.2, 74.2, 138.2; 3.56.4; 6.82.4, 8.43.3; cf. 1.16.

[97] Thucydides 1.68.3, 69.1, 98.4, 121.5, 124.3; 3.10.3-5, 13.6, 63.3; 4.86.1, 87.3, 92.4; 5.86, 96, 100; 6.76.2 and 4, 77.1, 82.3; 8.48.5. See *ATL* 3.155-57.

[98] Against Siewert, *Der Eid*, 91; see nn. 72 and 84 above.

[99] Thucydides 2.71.2 and 4; cf. n. 64 above; and 2.72.1.

[100] See above, pp. 6-8.

[101] See above, pp. 7-8.

[102] See above, p. 13.

[103] Compare Thucydides 2.71.2 (quoted in n. 64 above) with Mardonius' offer to the Athenians at Herodotus 8.140α and 143, as discussed above, pp. 15-16; cf. also p. 18.

[104] For the distinction, see Bickerman, "Autonomia," 326.

[105] See Thucydides 2.2.4; 3.61.2, 65.2, and 66.1; cf. n. 7 above.

[106] See above, n. 99.

[107] Thucydides 1.139.1 and 3, 140.3, 144.2; 4.86.1 and 87.5. Bickerman ("Autonomia," 319-24 and 331 with n. 53) does not consider the possibility of differences between the political vocabulary of 429 and that of 479 B.C. in his discussion of Thucydides 2.71 and 72.

[108] Thucydides 1.67.2: Αἰγινῆταί τε φανερῶς μὲν οὐ πρεσβευόμενοι, δεδιότες τοὺς Ἀθηναίους, κρύφα δὲ οὐχ ἥκιστα μετ' αὐτῶν ἐνῆγον τὸν πόλεμον, λέγοντες οὐκ εἶναι αὐτόνομοι κατὰ τὰς σπονδάς.

[109] Thucydides 1.139.1; cf. 140.3.

[110] Gomme (*HCT* 1.225-26) inclines to regard as a more likely reference the treaty by which Aegina agreed under duress in 457/6 B.C. to join the Delian League. His arguments have been convincingly answered by G.E.M. de Ste. Croix (*The Origins of the Peloponnesian War* [London, 1972] [= *OPW*] 293-94); one might add that the context of Thucydides 1.67.2, preceded as it is by the Corinthian complaint that the Athenians σπονδὰς τε λελυκότες εἶεν,

leaves little doubt that the Aeginetans, too, are thinking of the Thirty-Years' Peace. H. Schaefer (*Staatsform und Politik* [Leipzig, 1932] 167) believes αὐτονομία in the Thirty-Years' Peace to be the earliest occurrence "nach dem Stand der Überlieferung." This inference may well be right, but it is inconceivable that as loaded a concept as this would first have been coined for a formal treaty.

[111] Thucydides 1.97.1: "as leaders at first of allies who were autonomous and formulated policies in common meetings...." On the autonomy of the allies in 477 B.C., see the remarks of J. M. Balcer, *The Athenian Regulations for Chalkis* (= *Historia* Einzelschrift 33) (Wiesbaden, 1978) 5-7.

[112] Thucydides 5.77.5 and 79.1 with above, pp. 4-7, esp. 7.

[113] In this respect, it resembles the αὐτονομία of [Hippocrates] *Aër.* 16.19 and 35, and 23.27 (above, pp. 11-12); of the Median communities before Deioces at Herodotus 1.96.1, of pre-Thesean Athens at Thucydides 2.16.1, of the Thracian communities at Thucydides 2.29.2, 96.2-4, 98.3-4, and 101.3, and of some Sicels at Thucydides 6.88.4 (above, pp. 12-15). It is distinct from the αὐτονομία conceded by Xerxes to Athens at Herodotus 8.140α.2 (above, pp. 15-16), by the Greeks to Plataea at Thucydides 2.71.2 and 72.1 (above, pp. 16-22), by the powers contracting the Peace of Nicias to Delphi at Thucydides 5.18.2; and by Sparta and Argos to the Peloponnesian cities at Thucydides 5.77.5 (above, pp. 7-9).

[114] Aristotle, *Ath. Pol.* 23.5.

[115] Plutarch, *Aristeides* 25.1. For the form of the oath, see de Ste. Croix, *OPW*, 298-302.

[116] N.G.L. Hammond, ("The Origins and Nature of the Athenian Alliance of 478/7 B.C.," *JHS* 87 [1967] 41-61, esp. 52 and 55-56 [reprinted, with only minor alterations and under the title "The Organization of the Athenian Alliance against Persia" in the same author's *Studies in Greek History* (Oxford, 1973) 311-38, esp. 330 and 336-37]), referring to passages in which a subsequent loss of independence is either explicitly mentioned, e.g. Thucydides 1.98.4 and 3.10.4-5, or where it can be inferred from the context, e.g. Aristotle, *Ath. Pol.* 24.2 with Thucydides 1.115.3 and 101.3. It is worth noting, however, that none of these passages speaks of a loss of αὐτονομία.

[117] To this extent I agree with the thesis of A. Giovannini and G. Gottlieb ("Thukydides und die Anfänge der athenischen Arche," *Sber. Heidelberg. Philos.-hist. Kl.* 7. Abh. [Heidelberg, 1980]). I do not, however, follow them in denying the Delian League an existence separate from the Hellenic League even after 462/1 B.C. Surely, after the split between Athens and Sparta after Ithome it makes no longer any sense to regard the so-called "Delian League" as merely the Hellenic League under Athenian leadership. On this point, see also the account of Hammond ("Origins and Nature," 43-39). The following owes much to discussions with Dr. Michael C. Alexander.

[118] For the first of these motives, see Thucydides 1.95.1; the second can be inferred from Herodotus 9.106.3 and 114.2, and from Thucydides 1.89.2.

[119] According to Thucydides 1.95.1, these were οἱ ῎Ιωνες καὶ ὅσοι ἀπὸ βασιλέως νεωστὶ ἠλευθέρωντο. These are no doubt identical with οἱ ἀπὸ ᾿Ιωνίας καὶ ῾Ελλησπόντου ξύμμαχοι ἤδη ἀφεστηκότες ἀπὸ

βασιλέως, who are said at 1.89.2 to have remained with the Athenians for the siege of Sestos (sc. still under the auspices of the Hellenic League) after Leotychidas had removed the Peloponnesian from the allied force. Hammond ("Origins and Nature," 46-47) and R. Sealey ("The Origin of the Delian League," *Ancient Society and Institutions: Studies presented to Victor Ehrenberg* [Oxford, 1966] 233-55, esp. 243-44) contend that only the ethnic Ionians among the Asiatic Greeks are meant; but surely the addition of καὶ ὅσοι ἀπὸ βασιλέως νεωστὶ ἠλευθέρωντο at 1.95.1 must have included at least Aeolic Lesbos (see Herodotus 9.106.4), and probably other non-Ionians also; cf. *ATL* 3.227 n. 9; Gomme, *HCT* 1.257 and 271-72; and Meiggs, *AE*, 52.

[120] Thucydides 1.95.4: μετατάξασθαι; 95.6: οἷς οὐκέτι ἐφίεσαν οἱ ξύμμαχοι τὴν ἡγεμονίαν; and 96.1: παραλαβόντες δὲ οἱ Ἀθηναῖοι τὴν ἡγεμονίαν.

[121] Idem, 1.95.4.

[122] Idem, 1.102.4.

[123] For the possible exception of Plataea, see above, pp. 16-22. I do not agree with Giovannini and Gottlieb ("Thukydides und die Anfänge," 30, cf. 40-42) that the promise of the members of the Hellenic League in 481 B.C. not to go to war against one another (Herodotus 7.145.1) is tantamount to a guarantee of αὐτονομία for all members.

[124] So Meiggs, *AE*, 45-46.

[125] Thucydides 1.95.1: ἤν που βιάζηται, cf. 1.75.2: οὐ βιασάμενοι.

[126] Idem, 1.95.1: κατὰ τὸ ξυγγενές. That ethnic arguments were used is supported by the Athenian objection to the resettlement of the Ionians after Mycale at Herodotus 9.106.3, and by the role attributed to Aristeides in Aristotle, *Ath. Pol.* 23.4, cf. Diodorus 11.44.6. That this does not imply that only Ionians made the request has been argued in n. 119 above.

[127] Herodotus 8.3.2: ἀπείλοντο τὴν ἡγεμονίην τοὺς Λακεδαιμονίους.

[128] Aristotle, *Ath. Pol.* 23.4; cf. Diodorus 11.44.6.

[129] Plutarch, *Aristeides* 23.4-6.

[130] See H. R. Rawlings III, "Thucydides on the Purpose of the Delian League," *Phoenix* 31 (1977) 1-8.

[131] Explicitly stated by Thucydides 1.96.1: ἐκόντων τῶν ξυμμάχων, cf. 6.76.3, but implied also by Herodotus (loc. cit.), Diodorus (loc. cit.), and Plutarch (loc. cit. and *Cimon* 6.2-3).

[132] See especially the speech of the Mytileneans at Olympia, 3.10.3-11.3.

[133] Ephorus = Diodorus 12.4.5: ὧν ἐστι τὰ κεφάλαια ταῦτα· αὐτονόμους εἶναι τὰς κατὰ τὴν Ἀσίαν Ἑλληνίδας πόλεις ἁπάσας... Lycurgus 1.73 ...τοὺς δ' Ἕλληνας αὐτονόμους εἶναι, μὴ μόνον τοὺς τὴν Εὐρώπην, ἀλλὰ καὶ τοὺς τὴν Ἀσίαν κατοικοῦντας. Despite the fact that Suda, s.v. Κίμων, also speaks of τοὺς Ἕλληνας καὶ τοὺς ἐν τῇ Ἀσίᾳ, it is very doubtful indeed that the Greek cities of

Europe should have been mentioned, since at least one of these, Athens, was a contracting party to the Peace, whose αὐτονομία is more likely to have been taken for granted.

[134] Theopompus 115 F 153 and 154 (*FGH*).

[135] Meiggs, *AE*, 129-51 and 487-95.

[136] See O. Murray, "ʽΟ ἀρχαῖος δασμός," *Historia* 15 (1966) 142-56.

[137] Thucydides 1.113.4: "and all the rest became autonomous again."

[138] Idem, 1.108.3; Diodorus 11.82-83.2, with R. J. Buck, "The Athenian Domination of Boeotia," *CP* 65 (1970) 217-27.

[139] Bickerman, "Autonomia," 328 with n. 45. On the role of Thebes, see C. J. Dull, "Thucydides 1.113 and the Leadership of Orchomenus," *CP* 72 (1977) 305-14.

[140] Thucydides 1.139.1, 140.3.

[141] Idem, 1.108.4: ὡμολόγησαν δὲ καὶ οἱ Αἰγινῆται μετὰ ταῦτα τοῖς ᾿Αθηναίοις, τείχη τε περιελόντες καὶ ναῦς παραδόντες φόρον τε ταξάμενοι ἐς τὸν ἔπειτα χρόνον.

[142] Idem, 8.91.3, see above, p. 14 with n. 53.

[143] Idem, 3.39.2: νῆσον δὲ οἵτινες ἔχοντες μετὰ τειχῶν καὶ κατὰ θάλασσαν μόνον φοβούμενοι τοὺς ἡμετέρους πολεμίους, ἐν ᾧ καὶ αὐτοὶ τριήρων παρασκευῇ οὐκ ἄφαρκτοι ἦσαν πρὸς αὐτούς, αὐτόνομοί τε οἰκοῦντες....

[144] Andocides 3.14, where the γάρ should be noted in the clause: τὰς γὰρ πόλεις αὐτονόμους αἱ συνθῆκαι ποιοῦσιν.

[145] Thucydides 4.51, but cf. 6.85.2 and 7.57.4.

[146] Idem, 6.85.2, 7.57.4.

[147] Contrast Thucydides 6.85.2 with 7.57.4. For a possible explanation of the inconsistency, see Gomme-Andrewes-Dover, *HCT* 4.434-35.

[148] Cf. G.E.M. de Ste. Croix, "The Character of the Athenian Empire," *Historia* 3 (1954-55) 1-41, esp. 18-19.

[149] Thucydides 6.85.2, 7.57.4; cf. also 6.84.2-3.

[150] Idem, 5.18.2 with pp. 7-8 above, and 18.5 with p. 9 and n. 34 above.

[151] Idem, 1.96.1.

[152] Idem, 5.31.4 with Piccirilli, *Gli arbitrati*, 129-31; cf. above, p. 5 with n. 24.

[153] Thucydides 6.85.2; 3.46.5; 4.86.1.

[154] See n. 35 above.

[155] Scholars who believe this meaning to be primary are at a loss to cite relevant passages, e.g. de Ste. Croix ("Character," 20-21); Bickerman ("Autonomia," 324-25) cites no author earlier than Cicero. That αὐτονομία could be regarded as compatible with some interference in the judicial life of a state can be inferred from its juxtaposition with αὐτόδικος in the Peace of Nicias at Thucydides 5.18.2 (see above, pp. 7-8). The privileges which Samos received both in 412 and again in 405 B.C. in connection with her αὐτονομία are neither judicial nor legislative in character, but merely spell political self-determination in internal affairs: Thucydides 8.21 permits them to "run the city their own way" and handle the γεωμόροι as they saw fit; and ML, no. 94.15-16 (τοῖς δὲ νόμοις χρῆσθαι τοῖς σφετέροις αὐτῶν αὐτονόμος ὄντας) seems to envisage freedom to live by their own laws in terms of and as part of their guarantee of political independence from Athens. The same applies to the decree of 407 B.C. on the Selymbrians (ML, no. 87): if αὐτόνομος is correctly restored in line 11, it implies no more than political self-government, of which the clauses on hostages (8-10), cancellation of debts to Athens (12-14) etc. are simply concrete manifestations.

[156] Thucydides 6.84.3: "and as for the Chalcidians, whom he claims that we are illogically liberating here after having enslaved them at home, they serve our interest by having no armament and contributing money only, while here both the people of Leontini and all our other friends serve our interest if they are as autonomous as possible."

[157] See n. 149 above.

[158] Thucydides 1.69.5, 80.3, 82.5, 84, 99.3, 125.2; 2.11.4, 87.5; 3.4.2, 13.2; 5.9.6; 6.49.1, and the present passage.

[159] Idem, 3.39.2: ἐν ᾧ καὶ αὐτοὶ τριήρων παρασκευῇ οὐκ ἀφάρκτοι ἦσαν πρὸς αὐτούς, αὐτόνομοί τε οἰκοῦντες....

[160] Thucydides 1.105.2 speaks of πόλεμος; Diodorus, who mentions this war at 11.78.3-4 under 459/8 B.C., speaks of an earlier revolt (ἀποστάντας) at 11.70.2 (464/3 B.C.). For the improbability of the latter, see Meiggs, AE, 51 and 456.

[161] Cf. D. M. Leahy, "Aegina and the Peloponnesian League," CP 49 (1954) 232-43. The arguments of D. MacDowell ("Aigina and the Delian League," JHS 80 [1960] 118-21) that "Aigina was never a member of the Peloponnesian League but probably was a voluntary member of the Delian League from its formation," have been satisfactorily dealt with by Meiggs (loc. cit.) and by de Ste. Croix (OPW, 333-35). Cogent arguments against her membership in the Peloponnesian League have been advanced by T. J. Figueira ("Aeginetan Membership in the Peloponnesian League," CP 76 [1981] 1-24).

[162] Thucydides 1.97.1.

[163] See n. 131 above.

[164] Thucydides 1.96.1, Diodorus 11.47.1-2, Plutarch, Aristeides 24.2-4; cf. [Andocides] 4.11, Demosthenes 23.209, and Aeschines 3.258. The conventional rendering of χρήματα as "money" or "cash" has, to the best of my knowledge, never been challenged (see e.g. ATL 3.236-37 and Meiggs, AE, 58-60), and I shall adopt it here and in the following despite an uneasy feeling that it may be

too narrow and that it may have included also the contribution of "useful articles." Plutarch's story (*Aristeides* 24.1) that the Greeks assigned Aristeides the task χώραν τε καὶ προσόδους ἐπισκεψάμενον ὁρίσαι τὸ κατ' ἀξίαν ἑκάστῳ καὶ δύναμιν makes better sense if it is referred to the kind of resources each ally could offer and the quantity he could supply than if it is taken to refer to the ability of each to make monetary contributions. Not until the disjunction of χρήματα ἢ ἄλλο τι in the Spartan-Persian alliance of 412 B.C. (Thucydides 8.18.1) can we feel confident that χρήματα means "money."

[165] See p. 23 above.

[166] Thucydides 1.96.2; cf. also Antiphon 5.69-71, Andocides 3.38, and Xenophon, *De Vectigalibus* 5.5.

[167] Thucydides 1.97.1: "allies at first autonomous and making policy in common meetings."

[168] This can be inferred from Diodorus' report (11.47.1) of Aristeides' counsel to a "common" meeting of the allies to designate Delos as their "common" treasury.

[169] The most recent champions of this view are Hammond ("Origins and Nature," 51-52) and de Ste. Croix (*OPW*, 303-7).

[170] So J.A.O. Larsen, "The Constitution and Original Purpose of the Delian League," *HSCP* 51 (1940) 175-213, esp. 192-97; and idem, *Representative Government*, 58; *ATL* 3.138-41 and 227; V. Ehrenberg, *The Greek State*^{2} (London, 1969) 114; and, reluctantly, Gomme, *HCT* 2.264; Balcer, *Athenian Regulations*, 7-9; and P. Culham, "The Delian League: bicameral or unicameral?," *AJAH* 3 (1978) 27-31.

[171] Cf. Meiggs, *AE*, 460.

[172] Diodorus 11.47.1; cf. n. 168 above.

[173] Meiggs (loc. cit.) interprets Diodorus as envisaging a "Congress confined to allies," but that interpretation is not inevitable. For the oaths sworn by the Athenians as well as the allies, see Aristotle, *Ath. Pol.* 23.5, and Plutarch, *Aristeides* 25.1, with de Ste. Croix, *OPW*, 298-302.

[174] Thucydides 3.9-14, esp. 10-11, figures prominently in every discussion of the organization of the Delian League; see especially Hammond ("Origins and Nature," 57-60) and de Ste. Croix (*OPW*, 303-7).

[175] On this point, see C. W. Macleod, "Reason and Necessity: Thucydides III 9-14, 37-48," *JHS* 98 (1978) 64-78, esp. 64-68.

[176] Thucydides 3.10.3: ξύμμαχοι μέντοι ἐγενόμεθα οὐκ ἐπὶ καταδουλώσει τῶν Ἑλλήνων Ἀθηναίοις, ἀλλ' ἐπ' ἐλευθερώσει ἀπὸ τοῦ Μήδου τοῖς Ἕλλησιν. For the interpretation, see Gomme, *HCT* 2.262. For this aim of the Delian League, see K. Raaflaub, "Beute, Vergeltung, Freiheit?," *Chiron* 9 (1979) 1-22.

[177] Thuc. 3.10.4: μέχρι μὲν ἀπὸ τοῦ ἴσου ἡγοῦντο.

[178] Idem, 3.11.1: καὶ εἰ μὲν αὐτόνομοι ἔτι ἦμεν ἅπαντες... ἡμῖν δὲ ἀπὸ τοῦ ἴσου ὁμιλοῦντες....

[179] Thucydides 3.10.4: οὐκ ἀδεεῖς ἔτι ἦμεν.

[180] Idem, 3.10.5: "because so many had the right to vote, it was impossible for the allies to unite for self-protection, and they were enslaved, except for us and the Chians; but we participated in their campaigns, being autonomous and free in name only."

[181] On this last point, see Gomme, *HCT* 2.262.

[182] When League meetings were discontinued we do not know; the authors of *ATL* 3.228 believe it was "some while before 432 B.C.," but cf. also *ATL* 3.138-41.

[183] This possibility is suggested in *ATL* 3.140-41.

[184] Thucydides 5.18.5 with Gomme, *HCT* 3.669-70.

[185] We have already observed that Chios and Methymna are described as αὐτόνομοι (but not necessarily as the only αὐτόνομοι allies) by Euphemus at Thucydides 6.85.2, while only Chios, but not Methymna, gets that epithet at 7.57.4. At 6.69.3 and 7.57.3 and 7, on the other hand, only allies who were not members of the Delian League are called αὐτόνομοι.

[186] Thucydides 3.10.6.

[187] Idem, 3.11.1: "if we were all still autonomous."

[188] Loc. cit.

[189] Idem, 3.11.3: αὐτόνομοί τε ἐλείφθημεν οὐ δι' ἄλλο τι ἢ ὅσον αὐτοῖς ἐς τὴν ἀρχὴν εὐπρεπείᾳ τε λόγου καὶ γνώμης μᾶλλον ἐφόδῳ ἢ ἰσχύος τὰ πράγματα ἐφαίνετο καταληπτά.

[190] Idem, 3.11.4: "For at the same time they supported their claims by saying that, unless those against whom their campaigns were directed were guilty of some wrong, allies with an equal vote would not be willing to join in them; and on the other hand, they first kept leading the strongest states against the weaker, and, leaving them to the last when all the rest had been eliminated, expected to seize them weakened."

[191] Hammond ("Origins and Nature," 59-60 with n. 46) believes that this passage can be interpreted to mean that "the Congress in fact had the power of veto" over decisions taken by the Athenians. This has been effectively refuted by de Ste. Croix (*OPW*, 307). However, de Ste. Croix's own interpretation of ἰσοψήφους as having "the same weight in decision-making, the same power of effective decision" (ibid., 306) is not acceptable because in neither of the other two passages in which Thucydides uses ἰσόψηφος (1.141.6 and 3.79.3) is the weight of decision-making dissociated from the actual or potential casting of a vote. Cf. Plato (*Laws* 3.692a) where ἰσόψηφον surely does not refer to the collective vote of the Spartan gerousia, but to the vote of each of the twenty-eight γέροντες.

[192] Thucydides 1.99.2-3.

[193] See above, pp. 28-29.

[194] See above, pp. 23-26, 30-31.

[195] For these terms, see *ATL* 3.155-57, where the opposition of δουλεία to αὐτονομία (e.g. at Thucydides 4.86.1) does not receive sufficient attention.

[196] Thucydides 1.99.1: οἱ γὰρ 'Αθηναῖοι ἀκριβῶς ἔπρασσον καὶ λυπηροὶ ἦσαν οὐκ εἰωθόσιν οὐδὲ βουλομένοις ταλαιπωρεῖν προσάγοντες τὰς ἀνάγκας.

[197] Idem, 3.10.5.

[198] Idem, 1.98.4: "After that, they went to war against the Naxians, who had revolted, and reduced them by siege. This was the first allied state to be enslaved in contravention of established rules; later the same thing happened also to the other states one by one."

[199] Idem, 98.1-3.

[200] Herodotus 6.99.2; 8.66.2, 112.1-2, and 121.1.

[201] Thucydides 1.98.3: ἄνευ τῶν ἄλλων Εὐβοέων.

[202] This chronology, proposed by E. Lévy (*Athènes devant la défaite de 404* [= *Bibliothèque des Écoles Françaises d'Athènes et de Rome*, fasc. 225] [Paris, 1976] 277-79), is the most satisfactory, even though it does not take sufficient account of the synchronism with the flight of Themistocles (Thucydides 1.137.2, Aristodemus 104 F 10.3 [*FGH*], and Nepos, *Themistocles* 8.6 as opposed to Plutarch, *Themistocles* 25.2).

[203] Thucydides 1.98.1 and 2, 4 with *ATL* 3.155-57. On ἀνδραποδίζω, see P. Ducrey, *Le traitement des prisonniers de guerre dans la Grèce antique* (= *École Française d'Athènes: Travaux et Mémoires des Anciens Membres Étrangers de l'École et de Divers Savants*, fasc. 17) (Paris, 1968) 23-26.

[204] Plutarch, *Cimon* 8.3-7. Cf. A. J. Podlecki, "Cimon, Skyros and 'Theseus' Bones,'" *JHS* 91 (1971) 141-43.

[205] See Gomme, *HCT* 1.282.

[206] Cf. Thucydides 5.31.4, where enforced payment of tribute is irreconcilable with αὐτονομία; see above, p. 28; cf. also pp. 11-13.

[207] Thucydides 1.98.4.

[208] *ATL* 3.156-57, 228 with n. 14; Hammond, "Origins and Nature," 55; and Giovannini and Gottlieb, "Thukydides und die Anfänge," 30 n. 92.

[209] Meiggs, *AE*, 70, citing Gomme, *HCT* 1.282; see also de Ste. Croix, *OPW* 36 n. 69.

[210] See above, pp. 23-25.

[211] For the evidence for dating the revolt of Thasos ca. 465-463/2 B.C., see Gomme, *HCT* 1.390-91.

[212] See especially Thucydides 1.100-01. It remains a puzzle, however, why the allies were invited to participate in the settlement of 10,000 colonists at Ennea Hodoi. The most balanced modern account of the revolt of Thasos is that of Meiggs (*AE*, 83-86, 570-78).

[213] Thucydides 1.101.3.

[214] Ibid., 108.4, as discussed above, pp. 26-30.

[215] See above, p. 23.

[216] Samos also had to give hostages and pay an indemnity in installments,(see Thucydides 1.117.3, Diodorus 12.28.3-4, and Plutarch, *Pericles* 28.1); Mytilene did not have to pay tribute but had to accept 2,700 Athenian cleruchs (see Thucydides 3.50. 1-2).

[217] Thucydides 1.99.

[218] Ibid., 101.1-2.

[219] See, e.g., Herodotus 5.92α, Thucydides 1.18.1.

[220] Herodotus 1.152.3.

[221] Idem, 7.134-36, 104.4-5.

[222] Thucydides 2.8.4: ἡ δὲ εὔνοια παρὰ πολὺ ἐποίει τῶν ἀνθρώπων μᾶλλον ἐς τοὺς Λακαδαιμονίους, ἄλλως τε καὶ προειπόντων ὅτι τὴν Ἑλλάδα ἐλευθεροῦσιν.

[223] Idem, 1.67.2, 139.1 and 3.

[224] Idem, 4.86.1, 87.5, 88.1.

[225] Idem, 5.77.5 and 79.1, as discussed above, pp. 4-6.

[226] Idem, 1.101.2: κρύφα τῶν Ἀθηναίων.

[227] See above, pp. 26-30.

[228] The evidence on στρατηγοί, φρούραρχοι, ἐπίσκοποι, and ἄρχοντες ὑπερόριοι is conveniently assembled and discussed by W. Schuller (*Die Herrschaft der Athener*, 36-48 and 156-64).

[229] See ibid., 13-32 and 112-17. Fragments of a treaty between Athens and Mytilene, dated 427/6 B.C., seem to indicate that cleruchs were withdrawn from Mytilene and her αὐτονομία restored; see Tod, *GHI* 1², no. 63.12-13 and 18 (completely restored by B. D. Meritt; see *SEG* 13 [1956], no. 8) with Gomme, *HCT* 2.328-31. This suggests that the presence of cleruchs made αὐτονομία impossible. More cautious and agnostic is Meiggs, *AE*, 317.

[230] See Schuller, *Die Herrschaft der Athener*, 100-12.

[231] See ibid., 48-54.

[232] Thucydides 1.67.2, 139.1 and 140.3.

[233] Ibid., 139.1 and 3 with 140.3.

[234] Ibid., 144.2: "that we shall leave our allied states autonomous, if they were our autonomous allies when we made the treaty (sc. the Thirty-Years' Peace), and at the moment that the Spartans on their part give their own allied states the right to enjoy an autonomy determined by the wish of each and not by Lacedaemonian interests."

[235] For a more legalistic interpretation of this passage, see Bickerman ("Autonomia," 320-23). I am less confident than he that the last part of the sentence refers to "l'unité du régime oligarchique."

[236] Thucydides 2.71.2-4, as discussed above, pp. 16-22.

[237] Ibid., 72.1: καθάπερ γὰρ Παυσανίας ὑμῖν παρέδωκεν, αὐτοί τε αὐτονομεῖσθε καὶ τοὺς ἄλλους ξυνελευθεροῦτε, ὅσοι μετασχόντες τῶν τότε κινδύνων ὑμῖν τε ξυνώμοσαν καὶ εἰσὶ νῦν ὑπ' Ἀθηναίοις, παρασκευή τε τοσήδε καὶ πόλεμος γεγένηται αὐτῶν ἕνεκα καὶ τῶν ἄλλων ἐλευθερώσεως.

[238] See above, pp. 31-34.

[239] Thucydides 3.10.5 and 11.1-3. One wonders whether the aim of this desire was merely to have a free hand against Tenedos and Methymna (cf. ibid., 2.3), but that is not relevant to our problem here.

[240] Ibid., 11.3-4.

[241] Ibid., 39.2: νῆσον δὲ οἵτινες ἔχοντες μετὰ τειχῶν καὶ κατὰ θάλασσαν μόνον φοβούμενοι τοὺς ἡμετέρους πολεμίους, ἐν ᾧ καὶ αὐτοὶ τριήρων παρασκευῇ οὐκ ἄφαρκτοι ἦσαν πρὸς αὐτούς, αὐτόνομοί τε οἰκοῦντες καὶ τιμώμενοι ἐς τὰ πρῶτα ὑπὸ ἡμῶν τοιαῦτα εἰργάσαντο....

[242] Ibid., 46.5: τινα ἐλεύθερον καὶ βίᾳ ἀρχόμενον εἰκότως πρὸς αὐτονομίαν ἀποστάντα. Gomme (HCT 2.322) thinks that this would a apply to most cities other than Mytilene and Chios, because these did enjoy autonomy. But this is to take the Mytilenean argument concerning their own autonomy and that of Chios (3.10.5 and 11.1-3) too literally as historical fact. Diodotus' point is similar to that made by the Mytileneans: αὐτονομία exists for the allies in name only; even the ἐλεύθερον is in fact βίᾳ ἀρχόμενον. A similar point is made by Thucydides (7.57.7) in his own name, when he describes the contingents contributed by the Cephallonians and Zakynthians to the Sicilian Expedition as αὐτόνομοι μέν, κατὰ δὲ τὸ νησιωτικὸν μᾶλλον κατειργόμενοι, ὅτι θαλάσσης ἐκράτουν οἱ Ἀθηναῖοι.

[243] See the characteristics of Brasidas at Thucydides 4.81, esp. 1-2. Note particularly Brasidas' description as βουλόμενον and πλείστου ἄξιον Λακεδαιμονίοις γενόμενον which, as Gomme observes ad loc., was also said of Pericles at 2.65.4; cf. also δίκαιον καὶ μέτριον.

[244] Thucydides 4.85.1.

[245] Ibid., 86.1: "any allies that I should win for our side shall be autonomous; at the same time our purpose is not to have allies acquired by violence or deceit, but on the contrary to be your allies who are enslaved by the Athenians."

[246] Ibid., 87.5: "Nor again do we seek empire; but rather in our effort to stop others from exercising it we would do wrong to the majority if we would let you stand in our way when we are bringing autonomy to all."

[247] Ibid., 88.1.

[248] Idem, 5.18.2 with pp. 7-8 above.

[249] Thucydides 18.5 with p. 9 above.

[250] See the treaty between Corinth and Argos, proposed in 421 B.C. at Thucydides 5.27.2 with pp. 5-6 and 8 above, and the treaty between Sparta and Argos of 418/17 B.C. at Thucydides 5.79.1 with pp. 5-8.

[251] Ibid., 79.1 with p. 5 above.

[252] Idem, 6.77.1.

[253] Ibid., 84.3 and 85.2.

[254] Cf. n. 147 above.

[255] Thucydides 7.57.3-11; cf. 6.69.3 and 85.2.

[256] Ibid., 58.3.

[257] Idem, 8.21 with *IG* i^3. 96. If Samos was under an oligarchical régime from the time after her revolt until 412/11 B.C. (see A. Andrewes, *HCT* 5.45), the form of government in a given state does not necessarily have anything to do with its αὐτονομία.

[258] On this aspect of the decree, see W. Gawantka, *Isopolitie: Ein Beitrag zur Geschichte der zwischenstaatlichen Beziehungen in der griechischen Antike* (= *Vestigia* 22) (Munich, 1975) 178-97.

[259] ML, no. 94.12-18.

[260] Ibid., 17-18: καὶ περὶ τῶν ἐνκλημάτων ἃ ἂγ γίγνηται πρὸς ἀλλήλος διδόναι καὶ δέχεσθαι τὰς δίκας κατὰ τὰς συμβολὰς τὰς ὄσας.

[261] See above, pp. 7-8, 9-10.

[262] For this use, see scholion to Thucydides 2.29.2; I. Bekker, *Anecdota Graeca* 1 (Berlin, 1814) 466 s.v. αὐτονομουμένη πόλις; Cicero, *ad Atticum* 6.2.4; cf. 6.1.15, all as cited by Bickerman ("Autonomia," 324 n. 35). It is possible that two years earlier, Athens had guaranteed the autonomy of Selymbria, if the restorations proposed for ML, no. 87.10-12 are correct. If they are, the phrase [καταστέσασθαι δὲ Σελυμ]βριανὸς τὲμ πολι[τείαν αὐτονόμος τρόποι h]ότοι ἂν ἐπίστοντ[αι...] shows that the αὐτονομία is political rather than judicial. Cf. also n. 155 above.

[263] Thucydides 8.64.1-4.

[264] Ibid., 64.5, with the reading adopted in *Nomos*, 176-77: "so in Thasos the opposite happened of what the Athenians who were establishing oligarchy intended, and, it seems to me, that the same happened among many other subject states: for once the cities got moderation and immunity to pursue their own course of action, they progressed toward outright freedom, and showed no inclination for a putrid autonomy of Athenian provenance."

[265] See above, pp. 45-46.

[266] See pp. 25-26 above.

[267] See Meiggs, *AE*, 182-84; cf. also de Ste. Croix, *OPW*, 293-94.

[268] See above, p. 11 with n. 41, and 14 with n. 52.

[269] See above, pp. 42-43.

[270] See above, p. 43 with n. 242.

[271] See above, p. 45 with n. 253.

[272] See above, pp. 45-46 and 14.

[273] See above, pp. 45-46 with n. 262.

[274] For the date, see G. L. Cawkwell, "The Foundation of the Second Athenian Confederacy," *CQ* N.S. 23 (1973) 47-60.

[275] See above, pp. 23-25, 30-31.

[276] Diodorus 15.28.4: "all <allied cities> shall be autonomous, recognizing Athens as their leader."

[277] *IG* ii^2.43, most accessible in H. Bengston (ed.), *Die Staatsverträge des Altertums* 2 (Munich/Berlin, 1962) (= *SVA* 2) No. 257. The fundamental discussion of this decree is that of S. Accame, *La lega ateniese del secolo IV a.C.* (Rome, 1941) 48-69; for a good recent discussion, see J. Cargill, *The Second Athenian League: Empire or Free Alliance?* (Berkeley/Los Angeles/London, 1981) 14-47.

[278] *SVA* 2. No. 257.9-11: ὅπως ἄν Λακεδ[αιμό]νιοι ἐῶσι τὸς Ἕλληνας ἐλευθέ[ρ]ος [καὶ] αὐτονόμος ἡσυχίαν ἄγειν.

[279] Accame, *La lega ateniese*, 4-5.

[280] Xenophon, *Hellenica* 5.1.31; Diodorus 14.110.3. Cf. Cargill, *Second Athenian League*, 131-45.

[281] *SVA* 2. No. 257.19-23: "<each ally> shall have the right to be free and autonomous, governed by a constitution of his choice, without accepting a garrison, without receiving a resident archon, and without paying tribute." The same terms appear in the treaty by which Chalkis joined the Confederacy later in the same year; see *SVA* 2. No. 259.21-26.

[282] *SVA* 2. No. 257.25-46.

[283] On this point, see especially Accame, *La lega ateniese*, 53-61.

[284] See Isocrates 4.114 as cited by F. H. Marshall, *The Second Athenian Confederacy* (Cambridge, 1905) 20.

BIBLIOGRAPHY

A. *Books*

Accame, S. *La lega ateniese del secolo IV a.C.* Rome, 1941.

Adcock, F. and Moseley, D. J. *Diplomacy in Ancient Greece.*
London, 1975.

Balcer, J. M. *The Athenian Regulations for Chalkis* (= *Historia*
Einzelschrift 33). Wiesbaden, 1978.

Bekker, I. *Anecdota Graeca* 1. Berlin, 1814.

Bengtson, H. (ed.) *Die Staatsverträge des Altertums* 2.
Munich/Berlin, 1962.

Buck, C. D. and Petersen, W. *A Reverse Index of Greek Nouns and
Adjectives.* Chicago, 1945.

Cargill, J. *The Second Athenian League: Empire or Free Alliance?*
Berkeley/Los Angeles/London, 1981.

de Ste. Croix, G.E.M. *The Origins of the Peloponnesian War.*
London, 1972.

Debrunner, A. *Griechische Wortbildungslehre.* Heidelberg, 1917.

Ducrey, P. *Le traitement des prisonniers de guerre dans la Grèce
antique* (= *École Française d'Athènes: Travaux et Mémoires des
Anciens Membres Étrangers de l'École et de Divers Savants*,
fasc. 17). Paris, 1968.

Ehrenberg, V. *The Greek State*[2]. London, 1969.

Gawantka, W. *Isopolitie: Ein Beitrag zur Geschichte der zwischenstaatlichen Beziehungen in der griechischen Antike* (= *Vestigia* 22). Munich, 1975.

Gomme, A. W., Andrewes, A., and Dover, K. J. *A Historical Commentary on Thucydides.* 5 vols. Oxford, 1959-81.

Grote, G. *A History of Greece.* New ed. 4. London, 1888.

Hammond, N.G.L. *Studies in Greek History.* Oxford, 1973.

Jebb, Sir R. *Sophocles: The Plays and Fragments.* Part III: *The
Antigone*[3]. Cambridge, 1900.

Knox, B.M.W. *The Heroic Temper.* Berkeley/Los Angeles, 1964.

Kühner, R. and Gerth, B. *Ausführliche Grammatik der griechischen
Sprache*[3]. Hanover/Leipzig, 1890-1904.

Larsen, J.A.O. *Representative Government in Greek and Roman History.* Berkeley/Los Angeles, 1955.

_____. *Greek Federal States.* Oxford, 1968.

Lévy, E. *Athènes devant la défaite de 404* (= *Bibliothèque des
Écoles Françaises d'Athènes et de Rome*, fasc. 225). Paris,
1976.

Marshall, F. H. *The Second Athenian Confederacy.* Cambridge, 1905.

Martin, V. *La vie internationale dans la Grèce des cités (VIe - IVe s. av. J.-C.).* Paris, 1940.

Meiggs, R. *The Athenian Empire.* Oxford, 1972.

─────── and Lewis, D. *A Selection of Greek Historical Inscriptions to the End of the Fifth Century B.C.* Oxford, 1969.

Ostwald, M. *Nomos and the Beginnings of the Athenian Democracy.* Oxford, 1969.

Piccirilli, L. *Gli arbitrati interstatali greci* 1. Pisa, 1973.

Raeder, A. *L'arbitrage international chez les Hellènes* (= Publications de l'Institut Nobel norvégien 1). Kristiania, 1912.

Risch, E. *Wortbildung der homerischen Sprache*^{2}. Berlin/New York, 1974.

Schaefer, H. *Staatsform und Politik.* Leipzig, 1932.

Schuller, W. *Die Herrschaft der Athener im Ersten Attischen Seebund.* Berlin/New York, 1974.

Siewert, P. *Der Eid von Plataiai* (= Vestigia 16). Munich, 1972.

Tod, M. N. *A Selection of Greek Historical Inscriptions* 1^2 and 2. Oxford, 1946-48.

Vendryes, J. *Traité d'accentuation grecque.* Paris, 1904.

B. *Articles*

Bickerman, E. J. "Autonomia: Sur un passage de Thucydide (1, 144, 2)," *Revue Internationale des Droits de l'Antiquité*^{3} 5 (1958) 313-44.

Brunt, P. A. "The Hellenic League against Persia," *Historia* 2 (1953-54) 135-63.

Buck, R. J. "The Athenian Domination of Boeotia," *CP* 65 (1970) 217-27.

Cawkwell, G. L. "The Foundation of the Second Athenian Confederacy," *CQ* N.S. 23 (1973) 47-60.

de Ste. Croix, G.E.M. "The Character of the Athenian Empire," *Historia* 3 (1954-55) 1-41.

Culham, P. "The Delian League: bicameral or unicameral?," *AJAH* 3 (1978) 27-31.

Dull, C. J. "Thucydides 1. 113 and the Leadership of Orchomenus," *CP* 72 (1977) 305-14.

Figueira, T. J. "Aeginetan Membership in the Peloponnesian League," *CP* 76 (1981) 1-24.

von Fritz, K. "Die griechische ΕΛΕΥΘΕΡΙΑ bei Herodot," *Wiener Studien* 78 (1965) 5-31.

Giovannini, A. and Gottlieb, G. "Thukydides und die Anfänge der athenischen Arche," *Sber. Heidelberg. Philos.-hist. Kl.* 7. Abh. (Heidelberg, 1980).

Hammond, N.G.L. "The Origins and Nature of the Athenian Alliance of 478/7 B.C.," *JHS* 87 (1967) 41-61.

Larsen, J.A.O. "The Constitution of the Peloponnesian League," *CP* 28 (1933) 257-76.

_____. "The Constitution and Original Purpose of the Delian League," *HSCP* 51 (1940) 175-213.

Leahy, D. M. "Aegina and the Peloponnesian League," *CP* 49 (1954) 232-43.

Macleod, C. W. "Reason and Necessity: Thucydides III 9-14, 37-48," *JHS* 98 (1978) 64-78.

MacDowell, D. "Aigina and the Delian League," *JHS* 80 (1960) 118-21.

Murray, O. "'Ο ἀρχαῖος δασμός," *Historia* 15 (1966) 142-56.

Podlecki, A. J. "Cimon, Skyros and 'Theseus' Bones,'" *JHS* 91 (1971) 141-43.

Raaflaub, K. "Beute, Vergeltung, Freiheit?," *Chiron* 9 (1979) 1-22.

Raubitschek, A. E. "The Covenant of Plataea," *TAPA* 91 (1960) 178-83.

Rawlings III, H. R. "Thucydides on the Purpose of the Delian League," *Phoenix* 31 (1977) 1-8.

Sealey, R. "The Origin of the Delian League," *Ancient Society and Institutions: Studies presented to Victor Ehrenberg* (Oxford, 1966) 233-55.

Wüst, F. R. "Amphiktyonie, Eidgenossenschaft, Symmachie," *Historia* 3 (1954-55) 129-53.

INDEX LOCORUM

A. *Literary Texts*

Aeschines
  3.258   30 n. 164

Aeschylus
  Persae 50   20 n. 96
         242   20 n. 96
         745   20 n. 96

Andocides
  3. 14   27 n. 144
    38   30 n. 166
  [4].11   30 n. 164

Anecdota Graeca 1 (Bekker)
  s.v. αὐτονομουμένη
      πόλις   46 n. 262

Antiphon
  5. 69-71   30 n. 166

Aristodemus
  104 F 3.4 (*FGH*)   57 n. 79
       10.3 (*FGH*)   38 n. 202

Aristotle
  Ath. Pol. 23.4   24 nn. 126 and 128
             5   23 n. 113, 31 n. 173
          24.2   59 n. 116

Cicero
  ad Atticum 6. 1. 15 46 n. 262
                 2. 4   46 n. 262

Demosthenes
  23. 209   30 n. 164

Diodorus
  11.44.6   24 n. 126, 25 n. 131
     47.1   31 nn. 168 and 172
       1-2   30 n. 164
     70.2   30 n. 160
     78.3-4   30 n. 160
     82-83.2   26 n. 138
  12.4.5   25 n. 133
     28.3-4   40 n. 216
  14.110.3   48 n. 280
  15.28.4   48 n. 276

Euripides
  Heraclidae 1009-11 2

Herodotus
  1.27.4   20 n. 96
    95.2   16 n. 62
    96.1   12 n. 46, 16, 59 n. 113
    97.3-98.1   12

Herodotus
1.127.1	16 n. 62
152.3	40 n. 220
164.2	20 n. 96
169.1-2	20 n. 96
170.2	20 n. 96
174.1	20 n. 96
210.2	16 n. 62
2.102.4	16 n. 62
3.65.7	16 n. 62
82.5	16 n. 62
125.3	16 n. 62
4.93	20 n. 96
118.4	20 n. 96
133.2	16 n. 62
136.4	16 n. 62
137.1	16 n. 62
139.2	16 n. 62
5.2.1	16 n. 62
49.2	16 n. 62
2-3	20 n. 96
62.1-2	16 n. 62
63.1	16 n. 62
64.2	16 n. 62
65.5	16 n. 62
78	16 n. 62
91.1	16 n. 62
92α	40 n. 219
109.2	16 n. 62
116	20 n. 96
6.5.1	16 n. 62
11.2	16 n. 62, 20 n. 96
12.3	20 n. 96
32	20 n. 96
44.1	20 n. 96
45.1	20 n. 96
99.2	37 n. 200
106.2	20 n. 96
108	18 n. 75
108.1	18 n. 76
6	18 n. 76
109.3	20 n. 96
3-6	16 n. 62
123.2	16 n. 62
7.2.3	16 n. 62
51.2	20 n. 96
102.2	20 n. 96
104.4	16 n. 62
4-5	40 n. 221
108.1	20 n. 96
132.1	18 nn. 76 and 77
134.6	40 n. 221
136.2	2
139.5	16 n. 62
145.1	19 n. 87, 24 n. 123
157.2	16 n. 62
178.2	16 n. 62
202	18 n. 77
205.2-3	18 n. 77
235.3	20 n. 96
8.3.2	24 n. 127, 25 n. 131
22.1	20 n. 96

Herodotus
  8.50.2   18 n. 76
    66.2   18 n. 77, 37 n. 200
    100.3   20 n. 96
       5   20 n. 96
    101.3   20 n. 96
    112.1-2   37 n. 200
    121.1   58 n. 200
    132.1   16 n. 62
    140α   21 n. 103
    140α.2   15 n. 58, 59 n. 113
       4   15 n. 60
    142.3   16 n. 62, 20 n. 96
    143   21 n. 103
    143.1   16 n. 61
    144.1   20 n. 96
  9.2   18 n. 77
    28.6   17 n. 67
    40   18 n. 78
    45.2   16 n. 62, 20 n. 96
    48.2   20 n. 96
    60.1   16 n. 62, 20 n. 96
    67-68   18 n. 78
    86-88   18 n. 79
    90.2   20 n. 96
    98.3   16 n. 62
    106.3   24 nn. 118 and 126
       4   24 n. 119
    114.2   24 n. 118

[Hippocrates]
  Aër. 16.14-21   12 n. 43
          18   12 n. 44
          19   12 n. 42, 59 n. 113
          34-37   12 n. 43
          35   12 n. 42, 59 n. 113
          35-36   12 n. 44
      23.37   12 n. 42, 59 n. 113
          37-38   12 n. 44

Isocrates
  4.114   49 n. 284

Justin
  11.3.10   57 n. 49

Lycurgus
  1.73   25 n. 133

Nepos
  Themistocles 8.6   38 n. 202

Plato
  Laws 3.652a   64 n. 151

Plutarch
  Aristeides 21.1-2 17 n. 71, 57 n. 81
             2   20 nn. 91 and 95
            23.4-6   24 n. 129, 25 n. 131
            24.1   30 n. 164
              2-4   30 n. 164
            25.1   24 n. 115, 31 n. 173
  Cimon 6.2-3   25 n. 131
        8.3-7   38 n. 204

Plutarch
   Pericles 28.1   40 n. 216
   Themistocles 25.2   38 n. 202
   Moralia 864e   18 n. 77

Polybius
   9.39.5   57 n. 79

Sophocles
   Antigone 817-22   10 n. 38, 11 n. 41, 14
           875   11

Suda
   s.v. Κίμων   25 n. 133

Theopompus
   115 F 153 (*FGH*)   25 n. 134
        154 (*FGH*)   25 n. 134

Thucydides
   1.4   4 n. 13
     16   20 n. 96
     18.1   40 n. 219
       2   20 n. 96
     22.1   16
     41.1   3
     44.1   3
     67.2   1 n. 1, 23 nn. 108 and 110, 41 n. 223,
                         42 n. 232
     68.3   21 n. 97
     69.1   21 n. 97
       5   29 n. 158
     74.2   20 n. 96
     75.2   24 n. 125
     78   4 n. 13
     80.3   29 n. 158
     82.5   29 n. 158
     84   29 n. 158
     89.2   24 nn. 118 and 119
     95.1   24 nn. 118, 119 (*bis*), 125, and 126
       4   24 nn. 120 and 121
       6   24 n. 120
     96   35
     96.1   24 n. 120, 25 n. 131, 28 n. 151,
                         30 n. 164, 32
       2   30 n. 166
     96-97.1   30
     97   35
     97.1   23 n. 111, 25, 30 nn. 162 and 167, 32, 33
     98.1   38 n. 203
       1-3   37 n. 199
       2   38 n. 203
       3   38 n. 201
       4   20 n. 97, 37 n. 198, 38 nn. 203 and 207,
                         59 n. 116
     99   37, 40 n. 217
     99.1   37 n. 196
       2-3   36 n. 192
       3   29 n. 158, 37
     100-01   39 n. 212
     101.1-2   40 n. 218
       2   41 n. 226
       3   39 n. 213, 59 n. 116

Thucydides

1.102.4	24 n. 122
105.2	30 n. 160
108.3	26 n. 138
4	27 n. 141, 39 n. 214
113.4	26 n. 137
115.3	59 n. 116
117.3	40 n. 216
121.5	21 n. 97
124.3	21 n. 97
125.2	29 n. 158
137.2	38 n. 202
138.2	20 n. 96
139.1	1 n. 1, 22 n. 107, 23 n. 109, 27 n. 140, 41 n. 223, 42 nn. 232 and 233
139.3	1 n. 1, 22 n. 107, 42 nn. 223 and 233
140.2	4 n. 13
3	1 n. 1, 22 n. 107, 23 n. 109, 27 n. 140, 42 nn. 232 and 233
141.6	35 n. 191
144.2	1 n. 1, 4 n. 13, 22 n. 107, 42 n. 234
145	4 n. 13
2.2.4	22 n. 105, 51 n. 7
8.4	40 n. 222
9.4	42
11.4	29 n. 158
15.1-2	15 n. 54
16.1	13 n. 47, 59 n. 113
1-2	15 n. 56
29.2	13 n. 48, 59 n. 113
3	15 n. 57
63.3	14 n. 52
65.4	43 n. 243
71.2	16 n. 64, 17, 17 nn. 68 and 72, 18 n. 82, 21 nn. 99 and 103, 59 n. 113
2-4	43 n. 236
4	16 n. 64, 21 n. 99
72.1	17 nn. 69, 72 and 73, 18 n. 83, 19 nn. 84 and 85, 20 nn. 90 and 95, 21 n. 99, 43 n. 237, 59 n. 113
87.5	29 n. 158
96.1-4	13 n. 49
2-4	15 n. 57, 59 n. 113
98.3-4	15 n. 57, 55 n. 49, 59 n. 113
101.3	15 n. 57, 55 n. 49, 59 n. 113
3.2.3	43 n. 239
4.2	29 n. 158
9.1	3
9-14	31 n. 174
10.3	32 n. 176
3-5	21 n. 97
3-11.3	25 n. 132
4	32 nn. 177 and 179
4-5	60 n. 116
5	32 n. 180, 35, 37 n. 197, 42, 43 nn. 239 and 242
6	34 n. 186
11.1	32 n. 178, 34 nn. 187 and 188
1-3	43 nn. 239 and 242
3	34 n. 189
3-4	43 n. 240
4	34 n. 190

Thucydides

3.13.2	29 n. 158
6	21 n. 97
39.2	27 n. 143, 30 n. 159, 43 n. 241
46.5	28 n. 153, 43 n. 242
50.1-2	40 n. 216
54.3-5	20 n. 92
56.2	2
4	20 n. 96
4-6	20 n. 92
57.2-4	20 n. 92
58.1	20 n. 92
3	2
4-5	20 n. 92
59.1	2
2	17 n. 73, 20 n. 92
61.2	22 n. 105, 51 n. 7
63.2-3	20 n. 92
3	17 n. 73, 21 n. 97
64.1-3	20 n. 92
2	17 n. 73
3	17 n. 72, 19 nn. 84 and 85, 20 n. 93
65.2	22 n. 105, 51 n. 7
66.1	22 n. 105, 51 n. 7
2	2
67.2	20 n. 92
6	2
68.1	17 n. 72, 19 nn. 84, 85 and 86
5	18 n. 75
4.51	27 n. 145
81	43 n. 243
81.1-2	43 n. 243
85.1	43 n. 244
86.1	21 n. 97, 22 n. 107, 28 n. 153, 36 n. 195, 41 n. 224, 43 n. 245
87.3	21 n. 97
5	22 n. 107, 41 n. 224, 44 n. 246
88.1	41 n. 224, 44 n. 247
92.4	21 n. 97
97.2-3	2
98.2	2
8	3
118.1	3 n. 8
3	3 n. 9
8	4 n. 11, 53 n. 32
122.4-5	4 n. 12
5.9.6	29 n. 158
18.2	3 nn. 8 and 10, 7 n. 28, 12 n. 45, 15 n. 59, 17 n. 66, 28 n. 150, 29 n. 155, 44 n. 248, 59 n. 113
4	4 n. 17
5	9 n. 34, 28 n. 150, 33 n. 184, 44 n. 249
27.2	5 n. 23, 8 n. 31, 44 n. 250, 52 n. 21, 53 n. 22
29.1	5 n. 24
1-6	5 n. 24
2-5	1 n. 6
31.4	28 n. 152, 38 n. 206
33.1-3	5 n. 24
34.1	1 n. 6
49-50	51 n. 6
59.5	52 n. 21, 53 n. 22

Thucydides
- 5.77.5 — 4 n. 18, 5 n. 25, 6, 7, 15 n. 59, 23 n. 112, 41 n. 225, 59 n. 113
- 7 — 4 n. 19, 5 n. 25
- 79.1 — 5 nn. 20 and 22, 8 n. 30, 15 n. 59, 17 n. 66, 23 n. 112, 41 n. 225, 44 n. 250, 45 n. 251, 53 n. 26
- 4 — 6 nn. 26 and 27
- 81 — 8 n. 33
- 82.2 — 8 n. 33
- 86 — 21 n. 97
- 96 — 21 n. 97
- 100 — 21 n. 97
- 6.49.1 — 29 n. 158
- 58.3 — 45 n. 256
- 69.3 — 33 n. 185, 45 n. 255
- 76.2 — 21 n. 97
- 3 — 25 n. 131
- 4 — 21 n. 97
- 77.1 — 21 n. 97, 45 n. 252
- 82.3 — 21 n. 97
- 4 — 20 n. 96
- 84.2-3 — 28 n. 149
- 3 — 29 nn. 156 and 158, 45 n. 253
- 85.2 — 27 n. 145, 28 nn. 146, 147, 149, and 153, 33 n. 185, 45 nn. 253 and 255
- 88.4 — 13 n. 51, 59 n. 113
- 7.18.2 — 4 n. 13
- 57.3 — 33 n. 185
- 3-11 — 45 n. 255
- 4 — 27 n. 145, 28 nn. 146, 147 and 149, 33 n. 185
- 7 — 33 n. 185, 43 n. 242
- 8.18.1 — 62-63 n. 164
- 21 — 45 n. 257, 62 n. 155
- 43.3 — 20 n. 96
- 48.5 — 21 n. 97
- 64.1-4 — 46 n. 263
- 5 — 46 n. 264
- 91.3 — 14 n. 53, 27 n. 142
- Scholion to 2.29.2 — 46 n. 262

Xenophon
- *Hellenica* 5.1.31 — 48 n. 280
- 6.3.20 — 57 n. 79
- 5.35 — 57 n. 79
- *De Vectigalibus* 5.5 — 30 n. 166

B. *Inscriptions*

- IG i^3. 66.11 — 10 n. 37
- 96 — 68 n. 257
- 127.16 — 10 n. 37
- ii^2. 43 — 69 n. 277
- ML, No. 26.I.4 — 20 n. 96
- 27.6 — 18 n. 76
- 87.10-12 — 10 n. 37, 46 n. 262
- 87 — 62 n. 155
- 94.12-13 — 10 n. 37, 45

ML, No. 94.12-18	45 n. 259
13-15	45
15-16	45, 62 n. 155
16-18	45
17-18	45 n. 260
SEG 13 (1956), No. 8	66 n. 229
SVA 2, No. 257.9-11	48 n. 278
19-23	48 n. 281
25-46	48 n. 282
259.21-26	69 n. 281
Tod, GHI 1^2, No. 63.12-13, 18	41 n. 229
2, No. 204.31-33	18 n. 79, 20 n. 94
33-39	18 n. 80

www.ingramcontent.com/pod-product-compliance
Ingram Content Group UK Ltd.
Pitfield, Milton Keynes, MK11 3LW, UK
UKHW041425180426
11947UKWH00007B/302